SOCIAL MEDIA SUCCESS

Maximizing Your Online Presence (Practical Tips and Proven Strategies for Authors)

Dean Garman

ANish Publications

First Edition: 2018
Second Edition: 2024

Cover Design: ANish Designs
Publisher: ANish Publications
Published in the Islamic Republic of Pakistan

Disclaimer:

The information provided in this book is for general informational purposes only. While the author has made every effort to ensure the accuracy and completeness of the information, the author assumes no responsibility for errors, omissions, or inaccuracies. Any reliance you place on such information is strictly at your own risk. The author will not be liable for any loss or damage arising from the use of this book.

Trademarked names, logos, and images mentioned in this book are the property of their respective owners and are used here for identification purposes only.

Dedicated to all the passionate authors who dare to dream, create, and share their stories with the world. Your words have the power to inspire, entertain, and connect. May this book empower you to embrace social media, expand your reach, and make a lasting impact on readers worldwide.

"Social media is not just a spoke on the wheel of marketing. It's becoming the way entire bicycles are built."

- RYAN LILLY

CONTENTS

FOREWORD

In today's digital age, the power of social media to shape our lives and influence our choices is undeniable. As we understand the vast and ever-expanding world of online platforms, it has become essential for authors to understand how to harness the potential of social media to amplify their reach and connect with readers in meaningful ways.

In this foreword, I have the privilege of introducing you to "Social Media Success: Strategies for Maximizing Your Online Presence and Amplifying Book Reach." Authored by Dean Garman, this book serves as a comprehensive guide to help authors understand the complex world of social media and leverage its full potential.

Dean's expertise in the field, combined with his passion for empowering authors, shines through every page of this book. Drawing from years of experience and a deep understanding of the ever-changing social media world, Dean provides invaluable insights, practical tips, and proven strategies that will help you cultivate a thriving online presence.

From crafting an engaging author brand to selecting the right social media platforms, creating compelling content, and engaging with your audience, this book covers a wide range of topics essential for social media success. Dean's guidance will empower you to understand the challenges, tap into the opportunities, and build a loyal community of readers who are excited to engage with your work.

One of the standout features of this book is its ability to blend theoretical knowledge with actionable steps. Dean not only explains the principles behind effective social media strategies but also provides clear and practical advice that you can implement right away. Whether you are new to social media or seeking to enhance your existing presence, this book is an invaluable resource.

Furthermore, "Social Media Success" goes beyond mere tactics. It explores the importance of authenticity, genuine connection, and the power of storytelling. Dean reminds us that social media is not just a tool for promotion but a platform for building meaningful relationships and establishing your unique voice in the digital world.

I encourage you to look into this book with an open mind and a willingness to embrace the ever-evolving nature of social media. It is a powerful tool that, when used strategically, can propel your writing career to new heights. Through the pages of this book, Dean Garman will be your trusted guide, helping you understand the digital world with confidence and purpose.

I have no doubt that "Social Media Success" will be an indispensable resource for authors who are ready to harness the potential of social media and maximize their online presence. As you embark on this journey, I wish you success, growth, and the fulfillment of your writing dreams.

Ali W.

INTRODUCTION

In an era dominated by digital connectivity, social media has emerged as a powerful force that permeates nearly every aspect of our lives. It has revolutionized the way we communicate, share information, and engage with the world around us. For authors, understanding and harnessing the potential of social media is crucial in exploring the ever-evolving world of book marketing and promotion.

In this introduction, we explore the profound impact of social media on the world of literature and the opportunities it presents for authors to connect with readers on a global scale. We look into the transformative power of online platforms, the democratization of publishing, and the ways in which social media has reshaped the relationship between authors and their audience.

The purpose of this book is to equip authors with the tools, strategies, and insights needed to maximize their online presence and amplify the reach of their books through social media. By adopting the principles and techniques discussed in the following chapters, you will learn how to leverage various platforms effectively, engage with your readers, build a loyal following, and ultimately achieve your goals as an author in the digital age.

Each chapter will focus on different aspects of social media success, covering topics such as crafting an engaging author brand, creating compelling content, utilizing various social media platforms, understanding analytics, and exploring the challenges and opportunities that come with building an online presence.

It is important to approach social media not as a mere promotional tool but as a means of fostering genuine connections, sharing your passion for writing, and cultivating a community of readers who are eager to engage with your work. This book will provide you with practical advice, actionable strategies, and real-world examples to help you understand the dynamic world of social media marketing.

Whether you are a debut author or a seasoned writer, this book aims to empower you with the knowledge and confidence to embrace social media as a powerful tool in your author journey. It is my hope that through the insights and guidance provided, you will be able to understand the challenges, leverage the opportunities, and maximize the impact of your writing in the digital world.

Now, let us discover the strategies for social media success that will elevate your online presence and amplify the reach of your books.

Welcome to "Social Media Success: Maximizing Your Online Presence."

Dean Garman

PREFACE

Welcome to "Social Media Success: Strategies for Maximizing Your Online Presence and Amplifying Book Reach." In this book, I aim to equip authors with the knowledge, tools, and strategies necessary to understand the ever-changing world of social media and harness its immense power to expand their online presence and connect with readers on a global scale.

As an author myself, I understand the challenges and uncertainties that come with marketing and promoting a book in today's digital age. With the rise of social media platforms, authors now have unprecedented opportunities to engage with their audience, build a loyal following, and amplify the reach of their work. However, the abundance of platforms, algorithms, and trends can be overwhelming.

In these pages, I have compiled practical tips, proven strategies, and real-world examples to help you understand the complexities of social media marketing. From crafting an engaging online persona to choosing the right platforms, creating captivating content, and leveraging the power of influencer collaborations, each chapter is designed to provide actionable insights that you can implement immediately.

It is my sincere belief that social media can be a game-changer for authors, empowering you to connect with readers, cultivate a community of devoted fans, and ultimately achieve your book's fullest potential. By adopting the strategies outlined in this book, you can unlock new avenues of success and visibility in the digital world.

I encourage you to approach this book with an open mind and a willingness to embrace the possibilities that social media offers. Remember, building a strong online presence takes time, dedication, and experimentation. As you embark on this journey, I urge you to adapt the strategies to suit your unique author brand and writing goals.

I hope that "Social Media Success" becomes your trusted companion as you understand the world of social media marketing. May it empower you to harness the true potential of social media, reach new readers, and make a lasting impact with your remarkable work.

Wishing you success in your social media endeavors,

Dean Garman

PROLOGUE

In a rapidly evolving digital world, the role of social media in shaping our lives and connecting us with the world has become undeniable. It has transformed the way we communicate, consume information, and even discover new books and authors. As an author, understanding and leveraging the power of social media is no longer just an option—it has become a necessity.

In this prologue, we embark on a journey to explore the profound impact of social media on the world of books and storytelling. We look into the ever-expanding reach of digital platforms and the vast opportunities they present to authors like you. We witness the rise of self-publishing, the birth of online communities, and the democratization of the publishing industry.

As the digital world evolves, so do the strategies and techniques required to stand out in the crowd. In the following chapters, we will look into practical tips and proven strategies that will empower you to maximize your online presence and amplify the reach of your book. From crafting an engaging author brand to building a devoted community of readers, each page is filled with insights and actionable steps to help you thrive in the digital age.

However, it's essential to remember that social media is not a magic bullet. It requires time, effort, and an understanding of your target audience. It demands authenticity, creativity, and adaptability. The path to social media success is paved with challenges, but it is also adorned with incredible opportunities for growth and connection.

This book is your guide, your companion, and your source of inspiration as you understand the dynamic world of social media. It is here to remind you that you have the power to reach readers across the globe, to forge meaningful connections, and to make an impact with your words.

As you embark on this journey, I encourage you to embrace the possibilities, to experiment with different strategies, and to always stay true to your unique voice and vision. Remember that each interaction on social media is an opportunity to connect, to inspire, and to create a lasting impression.

Now, let us look into the strategies for social media success, where the digital world meets the boundless world of storytelling. Together, let's embark on this exciting journey and discover the remarkable potential that awaits you.

Welcome to "Social Media Success: Strategies for Maximizing Your Online Presence and Amplifying Book Reach."

CHAPTER 1: INTRODUCTION TO SOCIAL MEDIA SUCCESS

Understanding the Impact of Social Media on Book Marketing

Setting Goals for Your Online Presence

The Power of Building an Author Brand

Introduction To Social Media Success

Social media has become an integral part of our daily lives, both personally and professionally. With billions of users worldwide, platforms like Facebook, Instagram, Twitter, LinkedIn, and YouTube offer immense opportunities for individuals and businesses to connect, engage, and succeed. However, achieving social media success requires more than simply creating an account and posting content. It involves strategic planning, consistent effort, and a deep understanding of your target audience.

To build a successful social media presence, you need to start by defining your goals. What do you want to achieve through social media? Whether it's increasing brand awareness, driving website traffic, generating leads, or improving customer engagement, setting clear objectives will guide your strategy and help you measure your progress.

Next, it's crucial to identify your target audience. Who are your ideal followers or customers? Understanding their demographics, interests, and preferences will enable you to tailor your content and communication to resonate with them effectively. Conducting thorough market research and creating buyer personas can assist in this process.

Once you have defined your goals and identified your target audience, it's time to develop a content strategy. Consistency and quality are key here. Determine the type of content you will share—whether it's informative articles, engaging videos, inspiring images, or a combination of formats. Create a content calendar to plan and schedule your posts in advance, ensuring a regular flow of valuable content for your audience.

Engagement is crucial in social media success. Actively listen to your followers, respond to their comments and messages, and initiate conversations. Encourage user-generated content, such as reviews, testimonials, or user-submitted photos, to foster a sense of community and increase engagement. Use relevant hashtags, participate in trending conversations, and collaborate with influencers or complementary brands to expand your reach and visibility.

Analytics and data tracking are essential components of social media success. Use the available analytics tools provided by the platforms or third-party applications to monitor your performance. Analyze metrics like follower growth, post reach, engagement rate, and conversion rates to assess the effectiveness of your strategy. Make data-driven decisions and adjust your approach based on what works best for your audience.

In addition to organic content, consider incorporating paid advertising options offered by social media platforms. Paid ads can help amplify your reach, target specific demographics, and drive traffic to your website or specific landing pages. Experiment with different ad formats, targeting options, and budgets to find the most effective combination for your goals.

Finally, staying updated with the latest social media trends, algorithm changes, and best practices is essential for long-term success. The social media world is constantly evolving, and what works today may not work tomorrow. Continuously educate yourself, attend industry conferences, follow thought leaders, and adapt your strategy accordingly.

In conclusion, social media success requires a well-defined strategy, a deep understanding of your target audience, consistent content creation and engagement, data analysis, and a willingness to adapt to the ever-changing social media world. By implementing these principles, you can maximize your social media presence, foster meaningful connections, and achieve your desired goals.

Understanding The Impact Of Social Media On Book Marketing

Social media has revolutionized the way book marketing is conducted, providing authors and publishers with unprecedented opportunities to connect with readers, build an author brand, and promote books in a more targeted and cost-effective manner. Here are some key ways in which social media has impacted book marketing:

Audience Reach and Targeting

Social media platforms have billions of active users, allowing authors and publishers to reach a vast global audience. Through platforms like Facebook, Twitter, Instagram, and Goodreads, they can target specific demographics, interests, and reading preferences to connect with potential readers who are more likely to be interested in their books.

Direct Engagement

Social media enables direct and immediate interaction between authors, publishers, and readers. Authors can engage with their audience by responding to comments, participating in discussions, and sharing behind-the-scenes insights. This personal connection fosters a sense of community and loyalty, leading to increased book sales and word-of-mouth recommendations.

Content Creation and Promotion

Social media platforms offer various formats to showcase book-related content. Authors can share excerpts, cover reveals, author interviews, book trailers, and exclusive content to generate interest and excitement. They can also promote book signings, events, and giveaways to drive engagement and increase visibility.

Influencer Marketing

Social media influencers, such as book bloggers, BookTubers, and Instagram bookstagrammers, have gained significant influence in the book community. Collaborating with relevant influencers can help authors and publishers reach a wider audience, gain credibility, and generate buzz around their books through reviews, recommendations, and sponsored content.

Book Launch Campaigns

Social media provides a powerful platform for launching new books. Authors and publishers can create dedicated launch campaigns, utilizing platforms like Facebook Events or Twitter chats to build anticipation, organize virtual events, and offer exclusive deals or giveaways to drive sales and generate buzz.

Reader Feedback and Reviews

Social media allows authors to receive real-time feedback from readers through comments, direct messages, or online book clubs. Positive reviews and testimonials shared on social media can significantly influence purchasing decisions and attract new readers.

Data Analytics and Targeted Advertising

Social media platforms provide valuable analytics tools to track the performance of book marketing campaigns. Authors and publishers can measure engagement, reach, and conversion rates, gaining insights into the effectiveness of their strategies. Additionally, platforms offer targeted advertising options, enabling precise audience targeting based on demographics, interests, and behaviors.

Building Author Brand

Social media helps authors establish and strengthen their personal brand. By consistently sharing valuable content, insights, and expertise, authors can position themselves as authorities in their genre or niche. A strong author brand increases visibility, attracts loyal readers, and boosts book sales.

Global Reach and Book Discoverability

Social media transcends geographical boundaries, allowing authors to connect with readers worldwide. Authors can leverage hashtags, engage in discussions with international readers, and participate in global book communities, expanding their reach and increasing book discoverability.

In summary, social media has transformed book marketing by providing authors and publishers with powerful tools to connect with readers, create engaging content, build communities, and promote books effectively. By leveraging social media platforms strategically, authors can increase their visibility, foster reader engagement, and ultimately boost book sales.

Setting Goals For Your Online Presence

Setting clear goals for your online presence is crucial to ensure focus, measure progress, and achieve desired outcomes. Here are some steps to help you set effective goals for your online presence:

Define your overall objectives

Start by clarifying the broader objectives you want to achieve through your online presence. For example, your goals might include increasing brand awareness, driving website traffic, generating leads, expanding your customer base, boosting sales, or establishing thought leadership in your industry. Ensure these objectives align with your overall business or personal aspirations.

Make your goals specific and measurable

To set meaningful goals, make them specific and measurable. Instead of a vague goal like "increase social media followers," set a specific target, such as "gain 1,000 new followers on Instagram within six months." This clarity allows you to track progress accurately and determine success.

Set realistic and attainable targets

While it's essential to aim high, be realistic about what you can achieve within a given timeframe. Consider your available resources, time, and budget when setting your goals. Unrealistic goals can lead to frustration and demotivation. Break down larger goals into smaller, manageable milestones to make progress more achievable.

Establish a timeline

Assign specific timelines to your goals to create a sense of urgency and keep yourself accountable. Determine when you expect to achieve each goal, whether it's within a week, a month, a quarter, or a year. Having a timeline provides structure and helps you stay on track.

Align goals with relevant metrics

Identify the key performance indicators (KPIs) or metrics that will indicate progress towards your goals. For example, if your goal is to increase website traffic, relevant metrics could include page views, unique visitors, or referral sources. Make sure the metrics you choose align with your objectives and can be tracked effectively.

Consider your target audience

Keep your target audience in mind when setting goals for your online presence. Think about what you want to achieve for your audience. Are you aiming to provide valuable content, engage in meaningful conversations, or offer exceptional customer service? Aligning your goals with the needs and expectations of your target audience will help you create a more impactful online presence.

Review and adjust

Regularly review your goals and assess progress. Be flexible and open to adjustments if necessary. As you gain insights and data from your online activities, you may need to modify your goals or strategies to optimize results.

Celebrate milestones and successes

Acknowledge and celebrate milestones and successes along the way. Recognizing achievements not only boosts morale but also reinforces the value of your online presence efforts.

Remember that goal-setting is an iterative process. Continuously evaluate, refine, and set new goals as you progress and evolve in your online presence. By setting clear and measurable goals, you can focus your efforts, track your progress, and make the most of your online presence to achieve meaningful outcomes.

The Power Of Building An Author Brand

Building an author brand is a powerful tool for establishing your identity, connecting with your audience, and achieving long-term success in the literary world. Here are some key reasons why building an author brand is crucial:

Identity and Differentiation

Building an author brand allows you to define and express your unique identity as a writer. It helps you stand out from the crowd and differentiate yourself from other authors in your genre or niche. By cultivating a distinct brand, you establish a clear and memorable image in the minds of readers, making it easier for them to identify and connect with your work.

Trust and Credibility

A strong author brand builds trust and credibility with your audience. When readers recognize your brand, they associate it with the quality of your writing, expertise in your genre, and consistent delivery of value. This trust translates into loyal readership, positive reviews, and increased word-of-mouth recommendations.

Audience Connection and Engagement

An author brand provides a platform for connecting and engaging with your audience. By sharing your story, values, and insights, you create a sense of familiarity and relatability, forging a deeper connection with readers. Engaging with your audience through social media, blog posts, newsletters, and events fosters a loyal community that supports and advocates for your work.

Author Platform and Visibility

Building an author brand strengthens your platform—a combination of your online presence, followers, and reach. A robust author platform helps you gain visibility in the crowded literary world, making it easier for readers, publishers, and industry professionals to discover and engage with your work. A strong brand increases your chances of securing publishing deals, media coverage, and speaking opportunities.

Expanded Opportunities

An established author brand opens up new opportunities beyond book sales. It positions you as an authority and thought leader in your genre, allowing you to pursue speaking engagements, collaborations, teaching or coaching opportunities, and guest blogging. Your brand can extend beyond your books, leading to additional revenue streams and career growth.

Consistent Reader Experience

An author brand ensures a consistent and cohesive experience for your readers. From your book covers and author bio to your website design and social media presence, a well-developed brand creates a cohesive visual and emotional connection across all touchpoints. Consistency reinforces your brand identity and fosters a sense of trust and loyalty among your readers.

Long-Term Career Sustainability

Building an author brand is an investment in your long-term career sustainability. By cultivating a loyal fan base, establishing a strong reputation, and expanding your reach, you create a foundation for continued success. A well-established brand can help carry your career forward, making it easier to launch new books, attract readers, and understand the evolving publishing world.

In conclusion, building an author brand is a powerful tool that allows you to establish your identity, connect with your audience, and achieve long-term success. By developing a strong brand, you differentiate yourself from other authors, build trust and credibility, forge deep connections with readers, and open up a world of opportunities for your writing career.

CHAPTER 2: CHOOSING THE RIGHT SOCIAL MEDIA PLATFORMS

Exploring Different Social Media Platforms

Evaluating Platform Relevance to Your Target Audience

Tips for Platform Selection and Prioritization

Choosing The Right Social Media Platforms

Choosing the right social media platforms for your needs is crucial to effectively reach your target audience and achieve your goals. Here are some considerations to help you select the platforms that align with your objectives:

Identify Your Target Audience: Understand your target audience's demographics, interests, and online behavior. Consider the age group, location, profession, and interests of your audience. This information will guide you in selecting platforms that are popular among your target demographic.

Platform User Demographics: Research the user demographics of different social media platforms. Each platform has its own user base, with variations in age, gender, interests, and behavior. For example, Facebook has a broad user base across various demographics, while platforms like Instagram and Snapchat are popular among younger audiences.

Platform Features and Content Format: Consider the types of content you want to share and the features that best suit your needs. Some platforms, like Instagram and Pinterest, focus on visual content, making them ideal for showcasing images. If you plan to share videos, YouTube or TikTok might be suitable choices. If you prefer a text-based format, platforms like Twitter or LinkedIn can work well.

Platform Engagement and Interaction: Evaluate how users engage and interact on different platforms. Some platforms are more conducive to direct conversations and engagement, such as Twitter or Instagram comments. Others may be better suited for sharing longer-form content or fostering community discussions, like LinkedIn or Facebook groups.

Industry Relevance: Consider the social media platforms that are popular within your industry or niche. Research where other authors or professionals in your field are active. Engaging with relevant communities and thought leaders can help you connect with like-minded individuals and expand your network.

Time and Resource Availability: Assess your available time and resources to manage your social media presence effectively. Each platform requires time and effort to create and curate content, engage with your audience, and stay active. It's better to focus on a few platforms and do them well, rather than spreading yourself too thin across multiple platforms.

Platform Analytics and Advertising: Evaluate the analytics and advertising capabilities of different platforms. Access to insights and data is valuable for measuring your performance and optimizing your strategy. Additionally, consider whether the advertising options on a particular platform align with your goals and budget, as paid advertising can amplify your reach and visibility.

Experimentation and Flexibility: Don't be afraid to experiment and adjust your platform selection over time. Social media trends and user behaviors evolve, and new platforms may emerge. Regularly assess the performance of your chosen platforms and be open to exploring new opportunities as they arise.

Remember, it's not necessary to be present on every social media platform. Focus on the platforms that align with your goals, target audience, and resources. Quality engagement and consistent activity on a few platforms will yield better results than a scattered presence across numerous platforms.

Exploring Different Social Media Platforms

Let's explore some of the most popular social media platforms, along with their key features and audience demographics:

Facebook

Key Features: Facebook is a versatile platform that allows users to post text, images, videos, and links. It offers various engagement options, such as likes, comments, and shares. Facebook Pages are ideal for businesses, authors, and organizations to connect with their audience.

Audience Demographics: Facebook has a broad user base spanning various age groups and demographics, making it suitable for targeting a wide audience. It is particularly popular among adults, with a significant presence in all age ranges.

Instagram

Key Features: Instagram focuses on visual content, such as photos and videos. It offers Stories, IGTV, Reels, and carousel posts. The platform is highly interactive, with features like likes, comments, and direct messaging.

Audience Demographics: Instagram is popular among younger users, particularly those aged 18 to 34. It is widely used by individuals interested in lifestyle, fashion, travel, food, and creative content.

Twitter

Key Features: Twitter is known for its short-form posts called tweets, limited to 280 characters. It is a platform for real-time updates, news, and conversations. Users can retweet, reply, and use hashtags for engagement.

Audience Demographics: Twitter has a diverse user base, with active participation from professionals, journalists, influencers, and celebrities. It attracts users interested in current events, politics, technology, and entertainment.

LinkedIn

Key Features: LinkedIn is a professional networking platform focused on career development, networking, and business-related content. Users can connect with professionals, join groups, and share articles or updates.

Audience Demographics: LinkedIn is popular among professionals, businesses, and job seekers. It caters to a more mature audience, with a strong presence of working professionals, entrepreneurs, and industry experts.

YouTube

Key Features: YouTube is a video-sharing platform where users can upload and watch videos. It offers various content categories, including tutorials, entertainment, vlogs, and educational videos.

Audience Demographics: YouTube has a diverse user base, but it is especially popular among younger generations. It is widely used for entertainment, learning, and accessing video content on a wide range of topics.

Pinterest

Key Features: Pinterest is a visual discovery platform, where users can discover and save ideas in the form of images or "pins." It is popular for DIY projects, recipes, fashion, home decor, and travel inspiration.

Audience Demographics: Pinterest is primarily used by women, with a strong presence among users looking for creative inspiration, planning events, and exploring hobbies.

TikTok

Key Features: TikTok is a short-form video platform that encourages creative and entertaining content. Users can create and share videos with music, filters, and special effects.

Audience Demographics: TikTok is highly popular among younger users, especially teenagers and young adults. It has gained significant traction worldwide and is known for viral challenges and trends.

These are just a few examples of popular social media platforms. When choosing which platforms to explore, consider your target audience, content type, and your objectives for social media presence. Remember that each platform has its unique audience and features, so tailoring your approach to match each platform's strengths can help you maximize your engagement and reach.

Evaluating Platform Relevance To Your Target Audience

When evaluating the relevance of social media platforms to your target audience, consider the following factors:

Demographics: Review the demographic data of each platform to understand if it aligns with your target audience. Look at factors such as age, gender, location, and interests. Choose platforms that have a significant user base within your target demographic.

User Behavior: Consider how your target audience engages with different platforms. Are they more likely to consume video content, engage in discussions, or share visual inspiration? Understanding their preferences will help you select platforms that cater to their behaviors.

Industry or Niche Relevance: Research which social media platforms are popular among professionals or enthusiasts in your industry or niche. Joining platforms that are widely used within your field can help you connect with like-minded individuals and tap into relevant conversations.

Content Type: Determine the type of content you plan to create and share. Some platforms are better suited for specific content formats, such as photos, videos, or long-form articles. Choose platforms that support the content types that align with your strategy.

Engagement Opportunities: Evaluate the engagement features

and opportunities each platform provides. Do they allow comments, likes, shares, or direct messaging? Consider how these features can facilitate meaningful interactions with your target audience.

Platform Growth and Trends: Stay updated on platform trends and emerging social media platforms. While established platforms have larger user bases, emerging platforms may provide opportunities to reach a niche audience or get ahead of the competition. Be open to exploring new platforms that align with your target audience and goals.

Competitive Analysis: Research how your competitors or other authors in your genre utilize different social media platforms. Look at their strategies, content types, and engagement levels. This analysis can provide insights into platforms that are effective within your industry.

Resources and Time: Consider your available resources and the time you can allocate to managing your social media presence. Different platforms require varying levels of time and effort to create and curate content, engage with your audience, and stay active. Choose platforms that align with your available resources and allow you to maintain a consistent presence.

Remember, it's essential to focus on quality over quantity. It's better to have a strong presence on a few relevant platforms where you can actively engage with your target audience than to spread yourself too thin across multiple platforms. Regularly assess and analyze the performance of your chosen platforms to ensure they continue to provide value to your target audience.

Tips For Platform Selection And Prioritization

When selecting and prioritizing social media platforms for your online presence, consider the following tips:

Set Clear Goals: Define your goals and objectives for using social media. Are you aiming to increase brand awareness, drive website traffic, engage with your audience, or generate leads? Having clear goals will help you choose platforms that align with your objectives.

Know Your Target Audience: Understand your target audience's demographics, preferences, and online behaviors. Research which platforms they frequent and how they engage with content. Choose platforms that have a significant presence of your target audience.

Research Platform Demographics: Explore platform demographics and user statistics to ensure they align with your target audience. Look for data on age, gender, location, and interests. Platforms with a strong user base in your desired demographic are more likely to yield positive results.

Analyze Competitor Presence: Study how your competitors or authors in your genre utilize social media platforms. Identify where they have a strong presence and engage with their audience. Analyzing their strategies can provide insights into effective platforms for your industry.

Consider Content Compatibility: Assess the compatibility of your content with different platforms. If your content is visual, platforms like Instagram or Pinterest may be suitable. If you share long-form articles or thought leadership pieces, platforms like LinkedIn or Medium may be more appropriate. Choose platforms that can effectively showcase and support your content type.

Evaluate Engagement Opportunities: Look for platforms that offer engagement features that align with your goals. Consider whether the platform allows comments, likes, shares, or direct messaging. Engagement opportunities are essential for building relationships and fostering community with your audience.

Assess Time and Resources: Consider the time and resources you can dedicate to managing your social media presence. Different platforms require varying levels of time and effort. Prioritize platforms that align with your available resources, ensuring you can consistently produce quality content and engage with your audience.

Test and Monitor Performance: Start with a few selected platforms and monitor their performance over time. Track engagement metrics, reach, and audience growth. Based on data and insights, refine your platform selection and prioritize the ones that yield the best results.

Be Open to Adaptation: Social media trends and platforms evolve rapidly. Stay informed about emerging platforms and industry shifts. Be open to adapting your strategy and exploring new platforms that align with your goals and audience.

Quality Over Quantity: Focus on maintaining a high-quality presence on selected platforms rather than spreading yourself too thin across numerous platforms. It's better to actively engage and provide value to your audience on a few platforms than to have a diluted presence on many.

Remember that platform selection is not a one-time decision. Regularly assess your chosen platforms' performance and be willing to adjust your strategy based on audience feedback, trends, and changing needs.

CHAPTER 3: CRAFTING AN ENGAGING SOCIAL MEDIA PROFILE

Optimizing Your Bio and Profile Picture

Writing Compelling Descriptions and Taglines

Utilizing Keywords and Hashtags Effectively

Crafting An Engaging Social Media Profile

Crafting an engaging social media profile is crucial for attracting and retaining followers, creating a positive brand image, and encouraging audience interaction. Here are some tips to help you create an engaging social media profile:

Choose an Appropriate Profile Picture: Select a high-quality profile picture that represents your personal brand or author identity. It should be clear, professional, and easily recognizable even at small sizes. Avoid using logos or overly generic images.

Write a Compelling Bio: Use your bio to provide a concise and captivating description of yourself as an author or your brand. Highlight your unique selling points, genre expertise, or any notable achievements. Use keywords relevant to your niche to make it easier for users to find you.

Show Personality: Inject your personality into your profile. Be authentic, relatable, and genuine. Use a friendly and conversational tone to connect with your audience. Let your bio and posts reflect your voice, sense of humor, or values to create a more engaging profile.

Include Relevant Links: Share links to your website, blog, or other platforms where users can learn more about you or access your work. This makes it easier for users to understand and explore beyond your social media profile.

Utilize Visuals: Incorporate visually appealing elements into your profile. Use high-quality cover photos or header images that represent your brand or showcase your books. Include visually striking images or graphics in your posts to catch users' attention while scrolling.

Provide Value in Content: Share valuable and engaging content that resonates with your target audience. This can include informative articles, behind-the-scenes glimpses into your writing process, book recommendations, or thought-provoking questions. Aim to entertain, educate, or inspire your followers.

Use Hashtags Strategically: Research and use relevant hashtags in your posts to increase discoverability and reach a wider audience. Use popular hashtags in your genre or niche, as well as more specific or unique hashtags that align with your brand or campaign.

Engage with Your Audience: Actively engage with your followers by responding to comments, asking questions, and initiating conversations. Show appreciation for their support and encourage them to share their thoughts or experiences related to your content.

Maintain Consistency: Be consistent in your posting schedule to keep your audience engaged and build anticipation. Choose a frequency that suits your availability and resources. Consistency helps establish expectations and encourages followers to keep coming back for more.

Monitor and Analyze: Regularly monitor the performance of your profile using the analytics provided by the social media platform. Pay attention to engagement metrics, such as likes, comments, and shares, as well as audience growth and demographics. Analyze the data to understand what content resonates best with your audience and adjust your strategy accordingly.

Remember, an engaging social media profile is not just about self-promotion but also about building connections, providing value, and fostering a sense of community. Be responsive, authentic, and consistent in your interactions to create a memorable and engaging profile.

Optimizing Your Bio And Profile Picture

Optimizing your bio and profile picture on social media is essential for making a strong first impression and capturing the interest of your target audience. Here are some tips to help you optimize your bio and profile picture:

Bio Optimization

Be Clear and Concise: Your bio should convey your key message and purpose in a concise manner. Use simple and direct language to communicate who you are and what you offer as an author or brand.

Highlight Your Unique Selling Points: Identify your unique selling points and include them in your bio. What sets you apart from others in your field? Is it your writing style, genre expertise, or awards you've received? Highlight these strengths to grab attention.

Use Keywords: Incorporate relevant keywords in your bio to enhance discoverability. Think about the terms or phrases your target audience might use when searching for authors or books in your genre. This helps your bio appear in search results and attract the right audience.

Include a Call-to-Action: Encourage visitors to take action by including a clear call-to-action in your bio. This could be to visit your website, check out your latest book, sign up for a newsletter, or follow you on other platforms. Make it easy for people to engage with you further.

Show Personality: Infuse your bio with your unique personality. Share something personal or interesting about yourself that resonates with your target audience. This helps create a connection and makes you more relatable.

Profile Picture Optimization

Choose a Clear and High-Quality Image: Use a high-resolution image that is clear, well-lit, and properly framed. Avoid blurry or pixelated images that may create a negative impression. The image should be professional, yet approachable.

Reflect Your Brand: Your profile picture should align with your personal brand or author identity. Consider factors such as the genre you write in, the tone of your books, or the image you want to project. Ensure consistency across platforms for brand recognition.

Use a Close-Up: Opt for a headshot or a close-up image that allows viewers to see your face clearly. This helps create a sense of connection and familiarity. Avoid using group photos or images where you appear too small.

Maintain Consistency: Use the same profile picture across all your social media platforms. This consistency helps followers recognize you instantly and builds your brand identity. It also contributes to a professional and cohesive online presence.

Update When Needed: Consider updating your profile picture periodically, especially if your appearance or branding has significantly changed. This keeps your profile fresh and relevant.

Remember, your bio and profile picture are often the first things people see when they visit your profile. By optimizing them to be clear, engaging, and reflective of your brand, you increase your chances of capturing the attention of your target audience and encouraging them to explore further.

Writing Compelling Descriptions And Taglines

Writing compelling descriptions and taglines is crucial for capturing attention, piquing curiosity, and enticing your target audience to explore further. Here are some tips to help you craft compelling descriptions and taglines:

Know Your Audience: Understand your target audience's interests, needs, and preferences. Tailor your descriptions and taglines to resonate with their desires and aspirations. Use language and tone that speaks directly to them.

Be Clear and Concise: Keep your descriptions and taglines concise and to the point. Use clear and straightforward language that is easy to understand. Avoid jargon or complex phrases that may confuse or alienate your audience.

Highlight Unique Selling Points: Identify what sets you apart from others in your field. Whether it's your writing style, genre expertise, or a particular aspect of your brand, emphasize these unique selling points in your descriptions and taglines to capture attention and differentiate yourself.

Use Power Words: Incorporate powerful and descriptive words that evoke emotion and create intrigue. Choose words that are relevant to your brand or content and can elicit a strong response from your audience. Examples include "captivating," "inspiring," "unforgettable," or "mind-bending."

Create a Sense of Urgency or Exclusivity: Use language that creates a sense of urgency or exclusivity to encourage immediate action. Words like "limited time," "exclusive offer," or "available now" can generate a sense of FOMO (fear of missing out) and prompt your audience to engage with your content.

Invoke Emotion: Tap into the emotions of your audience by using words and phrases that evoke specific feelings. Whether it's excitement, joy, intrigue, or nostalgia, triggering an emotional response can make your descriptions and taglines more memorable and compelling.

Focus on Benefits: Highlight the benefits your audience will gain by engaging with your content or brand. Will they be entertained, educated, inspired, or empowered? Clearly communicate the value they will receive to create a strong incentive for them to take action.

Test and Iterate: Experiment with different descriptions and taglines to see what resonates best with your audience. A/B testing can help you identify the most compelling messaging and refine your approach over time.

Stay True to Your Brand: Ensure your descriptions and taglines align with your overall brand identity and values. Consistency across your messaging helps establish brand recognition and trust.

Be Memorable: Aim to create descriptions and taglines that are memorable and stick in the minds of your audience. Utilize catchy phrases, wordplay, or unique storytelling techniques to make a lasting impression.

Remember to adapt your descriptions and taglines to each platform or context, while maintaining consistency in your overall brand messaging. Regularly review and update your descriptions and taglines as your brand evolves or as you release new content to keep them fresh and engaging.

Utilizing Keywords And Hashtags Effectively

Utilizing keywords and hashtags effectively can significantly improve the discoverability and reach of your social media content. Here are some tips to help you make the most of keywords and hashtags:

Keywords

Research Relevant Keywords: Conduct keyword research to identify terms and phrases that are popular and relevant to your niche or industry. Use tools like Google Keyword Planner or social media analytics to discover keywords that your target audience is searching for.

Incorporate Keywords Naturally: Incorporate your chosen keywords organically into your social media content. Include them in your captions, titles, descriptions, and even in your bio. However, be mindful of not overstuffing your content with keywords, as it can make it appear spammy or unnatural.

Focus on Long-Tail Keywords: Long-tail keywords are more specific and targeted phrases that have less competition. They can help you reach a more qualified audience and improve your chances of appearing in relevant search results. For example, instead of using a generic keyword like "books," use a long-tail keyword like "mystery thriller books for young adults."

Location-Specific Keywords: If your target audience is location-specific, consider incorporating location-based keywords into your content. This can help you attract local followers or customers. For example, if you're promoting a book signing event in New York, use keywords like "New York book signing" or "NYC author event."

Hashtags

Research Trending and Relevant Hashtags: Stay updated on trending hashtags and industry-specific hashtags that are relevant to your content. Tools like Hashtagify or social media analytics can help you discover popular hashtags in your niche.

Mix Popular and Niche Hashtags: Use a combination of popular and niche hashtags in your posts. Popular hashtags have a larger audience but also face higher competition, while niche hashtags can help you target a more specific audience. Strike a balance to maximize your visibility and engagement.

Create Branded Hashtags: Develop unique hashtags that are specific to your brand or campaign. Branded hashtags help create a sense of community around your brand and make it easier for followers to find and engage with your content. Encourage your audience to use your branded hashtags when sharing related content.

Be Specific and Relevant: Use hashtags that accurately describe the content of your post. Avoid using generic or unrelated hashtags, as they may attract the wrong audience or dilute the visibility of your content. Use specific hashtags that are directly related to the topic or theme of your post.

Hashtag Placement: Incorporate hashtags within your caption or add them as a comment on your post. Experiment with different placements and monitor the engagement to determine what works best for your audience and platform.

Engage with Hashtags: Engage with other posts using the same hashtags by liking, commenting, or sharing. This can help increase your visibility and build connections within your community.

Research Hashtag Etiquette: Each social media platform may have its own hashtag etiquette. Research the best practices for using hashtags on the specific platforms you're targeting. For example, Instagram allows up to 30 hashtags per post, while Twitter has a more limited character count.

Remember to regularly review and refine your keywords and hashtags based on their performance and audience engagement. Stay current with trending topics and adapt your strategies accordingly. By effectively utilizing keywords and hashtags, you can expand your reach, attract relevant followers, and increase the visibility of your social media content.

CHAPTER 4:
CONTENT CREATION
STRATEGIES

Types of Content That Resonate with Readers

Creating Engaging Posts, Articles, and Visuals

Establishing a Consistent Brand Voice

Content Creation Strategies

Content creation is a crucial aspect of building an engaging and successful online presence. Here are some strategies to help you create compelling content:

Understand Your Audience: Gain a deep understanding of your target audience, their interests, preferences, and pain points. This knowledge will guide your content creation process and ensure that your content resonates with your audience.

Plan Your Content Strategy: Develop a content strategy that aligns with your goals and objectives. Outline the types of content you want to create, the themes or topics you'll cover, and the formats you'll use (e.g., articles, videos, graphics). Consider creating a content calendar to organize your content creation and ensure consistency.

Provide Value: Create content that provides value to your audience. Educate, entertain, inspire, or inform them through your content. Address their challenges, answer their questions, or share insights and expertise that are relevant to them.

Be Authentic and Unique: Infuse your content with your unique voice, personality, and perspective. Show authenticity and originality in your content to differentiate yourself from others. Let your passion and expertise shine through.

Mix Up Content Formats: Experiment with different content formats to cater to different audience preferences and capture their attention. Incorporate a mix of written articles, videos, infographics, images, podcasts, or live streams to keep your content fresh and engaging.

Storytelling: Use storytelling techniques to captivate your audience and create emotional connections. Weave narratives, personal anecdotes, or relatable stories into your content to make it more engaging and memorable.

Visual Appeal: Incorporate visually appealing elements into your content. Use high-quality images, graphics, or videos to enhance the visual appeal and catch the audience's attention while scrolling through social media feeds.

Incorporate Interactive Elements: Encourage audience participation and engagement by incorporating interactive elements into your content. Ask questions, run polls or surveys, conduct contests, or create interactive quizzes. This helps foster a sense of community and boosts audience engagement.

Repurpose and Recycle Content: Maximize the value of your content by repurposing and recycling it across different platforms or formats. For example, turn a blog post into a video or break down a video into shorter social media clips. This allows you to reach a wider audience and extend the lifespan of your content.

Stay Current and Relevant: Stay informed about current trends, industry news, and popular topics that are relevant to your audience. Incorporate timely and relevant content to keep your audience engaged and demonstrate your expertise in your field.

Analyze and Learn: Regularly analyze the performance of your content using analytics tools and insights provided by social media platforms. Identify which types of content perform best, which topics generate the most engagement, and adjust your strategy accordingly.

Listen to Your Audience: Pay attention to audience feedback, comments, and messages. Take their suggestions, questions, and concerns into account when creating new content. Engage in conversations with your audience to build relationships and understand their needs better.

Remember, consistency is key. Regularly create and share valuable content to maintain engagement and build a loyal audience. Adapt your content creation strategy based on audience feedback, industry trends, and the evolving needs of your target audience.

Types Of Content That Resonate With Readers

When it comes to creating content that resonates with readers, it's essential to understand their preferences and provide value. Here are some types of content that tend to resonate well with readers:

Blog Articles: Well-written blog articles that offer valuable information, insights, tips, or advice on topics related to your genre or niche can attract and engage readers. Consider sharing your writing process, book recommendations, author interviews, or behind-the-scenes stories to provide a unique perspective and cater to readers' interests.

Book Reviews: Readers often seek recommendations before deciding on their next read. Writing thoughtful and honest book reviews can help readers discover new titles, evaluate their choices, and engage in discussions. Share your opinions, highlight key aspects of the book, and offer insights that would help readers make informed decisions.

Author Interviews: Conduct interviews with authors, whether they are established or up-and-coming, and share them with your readers. Ask insightful questions about their writing journey, inspirations, challenges, and advice. These interviews can provide valuable insights into the writing process and allow readers to connect with authors on a personal level.

Writing Tips and Advice: Share your expertise as a writer by providing practical tips and advice to aspiring authors. Topics could include plot development, character creation, editing techniques, or ways to overcome writer's block. Readers who are interested in writing or are aspiring authors will find these tips valuable.

Behind-the-Scenes Content: Offer glimpses into your writing process, research methods, or the inspiration behind your stories. Share anecdotes, pictures, or videos that provide a behind-the-scenes look at your work. This type of content allows readers to connect with you on a more personal level and gain a deeper understanding of your books.

Exclusive Excerpts or Sneak Peeks: Share exclusive excerpts from your upcoming books or sneak peeks into your writing projects. This can create anticipation among readers and make them eager to read more. Be strategic in selecting engaging and compelling excerpts that leave readers wanting more.

Reader Q&A or Ask Me Anything (AMA) Sessions: Engage with your readers by inviting them to ask you questions or hosting live Q&A sessions. This interactive format allows readers to get to know you better, seek advice, and connect with you on a more personal level.

Writing Prompts or Challenges: Provide writing prompts or challenges to inspire and engage your readers. Encourage them to participate by writing their own stories based on the prompts or challenges you provide. This fosters a sense of community and allows readers to showcase their creativity.

Inspirational or Motivational Content: Share inspirational quotes, stories, or messages that resonate with readers on a deeper level. Offer encouragement, motivation, or insights into the writing journey. This type of content can inspire and uplift readers, creating a positive connection with your brand.

Collaborations or Guest Posts: Collaborate with other authors, bloggers, or influencers in your niche. Guest posts or joint projects can introduce you to new audiences and offer diverse perspectives to your readers. It also allows you to tap into their expertise and extend your reach.

Remember, it's important to balance promotional content with content that provides value to readers. By focusing on content that educates, entertains, and engages, you can build a loyal and engaged readership who eagerly awaits your next creation.

Creating Engaging Posts, Articles, And Visuals

Creating engaging posts, articles, and visuals is essential for capturing and maintaining the attention of your audience. Here are some tips to help you create compelling content across different formats:

Engaging Posts

Start with a Strong Hook: Grab the reader's attention from the beginning with a captivating hook. Pose a question, make a bold statement, or share an intriguing fact to entice readers to continue reading.

Keep it Concise: Social media posts should be concise and to the point. Use clear and compelling language to deliver your message effectively. Keep sentences short and paragraphs brief to maintain readability.

Use Visuals: Incorporate eye-catching visuals, such as high-quality images, GIFs, or videos, to enhance your posts. Visuals can help tell a story, evoke emotions, and attract attention as users scroll through their feeds.

Include a Call to Action (CTA): Encourage your audience to take action by including a clear and specific CTA. Whether it's asking them to like, comment, share, visit your website, or purchase your book, a CTA prompts engagement and guides readers on the next step.

Engaging Articles

Craft an Attention-Grabbing Headline: Create a headline that instantly captures the reader's interest and makes them want to click and read more. Use power words, numbers, and a sense of urgency or curiosity to make your headline compelling.

Start with a Strong Introduction: The introduction should hook the reader and provide a clear overview of what they can expect from the article. Engage them with an interesting anecdote, a thought-provoking question, or a captivating story.

Provide Value and Engaging Content: Focus on delivering value to your readers by offering practical advice, insightful analysis, or entertaining stories. Keep your content engaging by using a conversational tone, including storytelling elements, and breaking up the text with subheadings, bullet points, and images.

Incorporate Visuals: Visuals play a crucial role in articles as well. Include relevant images, infographics, or graphs to enhance understanding and break up the text. Visuals also make your articles more shareable on social media platforms.

Engaging Visuals

Use High-Quality Images: Choose visually appealing and high-resolution images that are relevant to your content. Ensure that the images are clear, visually striking, and aligned with your brand identity.

Infographics and Data Visualization: Present information in a visually appealing and easy-to-digest format by creating infographics or visualizing data. Use charts, graphs, or diagrams to convey complex information in a visually engaging way.

Incorporate Branding Elements: Include your brand's logo, colors, and fonts in your visuals to reinforce your brand identity. Consistent branding across visuals helps in building brand recognition and establishes a cohesive visual presence.

Experiment with Different Formats: Explore different visual formats such as quote graphics, illustrations, collages, or animated visuals to add variety to your content. Mix up static and dynamic visuals to keep your audience engaged.

Add Captions or Text Overlay: Enhance the impact of your visuals by adding captions, quotes, or text overlay. This can help provide context, highlight key points, or spark curiosity.

Optimize for Platform Requirements: Different social media platforms have different requirements for visuals. Be mindful of the recommended dimensions, aspect ratios, and file sizes to ensure your visuals appear well on each platform.

Remember to tailor your content and visuals to your target audience's preferences, interests, and the platform you're using. Analyze the engagement metrics and feedback from your audience to refine your content creation strategies and continually improve the engagement levels of your posts, articles, and visuals.

Establishing A Consistent Brand Voice

Establishing a consistent brand voice is crucial for creating a recognizable and cohesive brand identity across your online presence. Here are some steps to help you establish a consistent brand voice:

Define Your Brand Personality: Start by defining the personality and characteristics you want your brand to portray. Is your brand playful, authoritative, friendly, or sophisticated? Consider your target audience and what resonates with them. This will lay the foundation for your brand voice.

Understand Your Audience: Gain a deep understanding of your target audience's preferences, values, and communication style. This will help you tailor your brand voice to resonate with them. Consider the language, tone, and style that your audience responds well to.

Develop Brand Guidelines: Create brand guidelines that outline the key elements of your brand voice. Include guidelines on tone, language style, vocabulary, and any specific do's and don'ts. These guidelines will serve as a reference for you and your team to maintain consistency in your communication.

Be Authentic and Consistent: Your brand voice should align with your brand's values and be authentic. Consistency is key in maintaining a recognizable brand voice across different channels and platforms. Ensure that your brand voice remains consistent in your website copy, social media posts, blog articles, email communications, and any other touchpoints with your audience.

Use a Conversational Tone: Consider adopting a conversational tone in your brand voice, unless your brand requires a more formal or professional approach. This helps create a relatable and approachable persona. Write as if you are having a conversation with your audience, using language and expressions that they can connect with.

Use Language that Reflects Your Brand's Values: Choose language that reflects your brand's values and resonates with your audience. If your brand is known for being innovative and forward-thinking, use language that conveys that sense of innovation. If your brand is focused on empathy and inclusivity, use language that is inclusive and empathetic.

Be Mindful of Cultural Sensitivity: In a globalized world, it's important to be mindful of cultural sensitivity in your brand voice. Avoid using language or references that could be offensive or misunderstood by different cultures or communities. Conduct research and be aware of cultural nuances when communicating with diverse audiences.

Train Your Team: If you have a team that manages your brand's communication, provide them with proper training on your brand voice guidelines. Ensure that everyone understands and embodies the desired brand voice when interacting with your audience.

Evolve and Adapt: Your brand voice may evolve over time as your brand grows and your audience changes. Stay attuned to feedback and trends in your industry, and be willing to adapt your brand voice accordingly. However, ensure that any changes remain consistent with your brand's core values and identity.

Remember, establishing a consistent brand voice takes time and effort. Stay true to your brand's identity and continuously evaluate and refine your communication to ensure that it resonates with your audience and supports your overall brand goals.

CHAPTER 5: BUILDING AND ENGAGING YOUR ONLINE COMMUNITY

Growing Your Social Media Following

Encouraging Interaction and Conversation

Leveraging User-Generated Content

Building And Engaging Your Online Community

Building and engaging an online community is a valuable strategy for fostering relationships, expanding your reach, and cultivating a loyal audience. Here are some tips to help you build and engage your online community:

Define Your Community: Identify the target audience or niche that you want to build a community around. Understand their interests, needs, and pain points. This clarity will help you tailor your content and engagement strategies to resonate with your community members.

Choose the Right Platforms: Select the social media platforms or online forums where your target audience is most active. Focus your efforts on these platforms to maximize your reach and engagement potential. Each platform has its own unique features and community dynamics, so adapt your approach accordingly.

Consistent and Valuable Content: Regularly provide valuable content that addresses the interests and needs of your community. This can include informative articles, engaging videos, inspiring stories, or interactive discussions. Consistency in posting builds trust and keeps your community engaged.

Foster Two-Way Communication: Encourage and actively participate in conversations with your community. Respond to comments, messages, and inquiries in a timely manner. Ask questions, seek feedback, and create opportunities for community members to share their thoughts and experiences. Make your community feel heard and valued.

Create a Sense of Belonging: Cultivate a sense of belonging and inclusivity within your community. Make community members feel like they are part of something special by using inclusive language, acknowledging their contributions, and celebrating their achievements. Encourage members to engage with one another and foster a supportive environment.

Organize Events and Challenges: Plan and host events or challenges that encourage community participation. This could include live Q&A sessions, virtual book clubs, writing prompts, contests, or giveaways. These activities foster interaction, build excitement, and create shared experiences within your community.

Collaborate with Influencers or Experts: Collaborate with influencers or experts in your niche to provide additional value to your community. Invite them to share their insights, conduct interviews, or host joint events. This expands your reach, brings fresh perspectives, and adds credibility to your community.

Encourage User-Generated Content: Motivate your community members to generate and share their own content related to your brand or community. This could involve sharing their reviews, fan art, book recommendations, or personal stories. User-generated content not only creates engagement but also strengthens the bond among community members.

Offer Exclusive Benefits: Provide exclusive benefits or rewards to your community members to make them feel special. This could include early access to content, special discounts, exclusive merchandise, or access to private groups or forums. Rewarding your community fosters loyalty and encourages ongoing engagement.

Monitor and Analyze Community Insights: Regularly monitor and analyze community insights and engagement metrics. Pay attention to what content resonates most with your community, which activities generate the most participation, and how the community evolves over time. Use this data to refine your strategies and better serve your community.

Remember, building and engaging an online community takes time and effort. Be patient, genuine, and consistent in your interactions. The more value you provide and the stronger the connections you build, the more vibrant and engaged your online community will become.

Growing Your Social Media Following

Growing your social media following is an important aspect of building your online presence and expanding your reach. Here are some tips to help you grow your social media following:

Know Your Target Audience: Understand your target audience's demographics, interests, and preferences. Tailor your content and engagement strategies to resonate with them effectively.

Consistent and Quality Content: Post consistently and provide high-quality content that aligns with your audience's interests. Focus on delivering value, whether it's through informative articles, entertaining videos, inspiring quotes, or engaging discussions.

Use Relevant Hashtags: Research and use relevant hashtags in your posts to increase discoverability. Hashtags help users find content related to specific topics or interests, allowing you to reach a wider audience.

Engage with Your Audience: Actively engage with your audience by responding to comments, messages, and mentions. Show genuine interest in their thoughts, questions, and feedback. Engaging with your audience builds relationships and encourages them to become loyal followers.

Cross-Promote: Promote your social media accounts across different platforms, such as including links in your email signature, blog posts, website, or other social media profiles. Cross-promoting helps channel your existing audience to your social media platforms.

Collaborate with Others: Collaborate with influencers, authors, or brands in your niche to reach their audience. Guest post on their blogs, participate in joint giveaways or interviews, or create content together. Collaborations expose you to new audiences and provide opportunities for mutual growth.

Run Contests or Giveaways: Organize contests or giveaways on your social media platforms. Encourage followers to participate by liking, sharing, or commenting on your posts. This helps increase engagement and attract new followers who are interested in winning the prize.

Leverage Influencer Marketing: Partner with influencers or micro-influencers in your niche to promote your social media accounts or content. Their endorsements can introduce your brand to their followers, helping you gain visibility and followers.

Utilize Paid Advertising: Consider investing in paid advertising on social media platforms. Target your ads to specific demographics or interests relevant to your target audience. Paid advertising can help you reach a larger audience and accelerate your follower growth.

Analyze and Optimize: Continuously analyze your social media performance using platform analytics and third-party tools. Understand which content performs best, what times of day or week are optimal for engagement, and which strategies yield the most growth. Use this data to optimize your approach and refine your content and engagement strategies.

Remember, building a genuine and engaged following takes time and effort. Focus on building relationships, providing value, and staying consistent. As your following grows, nurture your community and continue to engage with your audience to foster loyalty and create a thriving social media presence.

Encouraging Interaction And Conversation

Encouraging interaction and conversation on social media is crucial for fostering engagement and building a thriving online community. Here are some tips to encourage interaction and conversation with your audience:

Ask Questions: Pose thought-provoking questions in your social media posts to encourage your audience to share their thoughts and opinions. Ask open-ended questions that invite conversation and make your audience feel involved.

Respond Promptly: Be responsive to comments, messages, and mentions from your audience. Show genuine interest in their feedback and questions by providing timely and thoughtful responses. This demonstrates that you value their engagement and encourages further interaction.

Run Polls and Surveys: Utilize the polling feature available on various social media platforms to gather opinions from your audience. Polls are an effective way to engage your audience and spark conversations around specific topics or preferences.

Host Q&A Sessions: Schedule regular Q&A sessions where your audience can ask you questions about your books, writing process, or any relevant topic. This creates a space for meaningful conversation and allows your audience to connect with you on a more personal level.

Encourage User-Generated Content: Motivate your audience to create and share their own content related to your brand or books. This can include fan art, book reviews, or personal stories. Repost or share user-generated content, giving credit to the creators and fostering a sense of community and appreciation.

Create Discussion Topics: Start conversations by posting about current trends, industry news, or topics related to your books. Share your thoughts and invite your audience to share theirs. Encourage respectful and constructive discussions within the comments section.

Engage in Social Listening: Monitor conversations related to your brand or industry on social media. Look for opportunities to join relevant discussions, provide insights, and engage with users who are talking about your books or topics of interest. This demonstrates your active presence and willingness to engage with your audience.

Organize Live Sessions: Host live sessions such as Facebook Live, Instagram Live, or Twitter Spaces, where you can interact with your audience in real-time. Use these sessions to answer questions, share updates, or conduct interviews. Live sessions create an interactive and immediate platform for engagement.

Create Contests or Challenges: Organize contests or challenges that require participation from your audience. Encourage them to share their entries or experiences, fostering interaction and creating a sense of friendly competition. Offer incentives such as prizes or shoutouts to further motivate participation.

Foster a Positive and Inclusive Environment: Create a welcoming and inclusive atmosphere where your audience feels comfortable engaging with one another. Set clear guidelines for respectful behavior and moderate discussions to ensure a safe and supportive space for conversation.

Remember, authentic and meaningful engagement is key. Take the time to listen, respond, and show appreciation for your audience's contributions. By fostering interaction and conversation, you not only strengthen your relationship with your audience but also create a vibrant and engaged community around your brand and books.

Leveraging User-Generated Content

Leveraging user-generated content (UGC) is a powerful way to engage your audience, showcase their creativity, and build a strong sense of community. Here are some tips for effectively leveraging user-generated content:

Encourage and Inspire: Create opportunities for your audience to contribute UGC by encouraging them to share their experiences, thoughts, or creations related to your brand or books. Inspire them by providing clear prompts or challenges that align with your brand values and interests.

Create a Hashtag: Develop a unique hashtag that represents your brand or a specific campaign. Encourage your audience to use the hashtag when sharing their content, allowing you to easily discover and track UGC. Feature the best UGC on your social media platforms or website to showcase your audience's contributions.

Repost and Share: When you come across compelling UGC, ask for permission from the creator to repost or share it on your social media channels. Highlight the creativity, passion, or unique perspective of your audience. This not only recognizes their efforts but also encourages others to contribute their own content.

Run UGC Campaigns: Launch specific UGC campaigns or contests that motivate your audience to create and share content. For example, ask them to submit book reviews, fan art, or creative interpretations of your characters. Offer incentives such as prizes or shoutouts to encourage participation.

Showcase UGC on Your Website: Create a dedicated section on your website or blog to showcase UGC. Curate the best submissions, with proper attribution, and display them as a way to celebrate and recognize your audience. This can serve as a source of inspiration for others and foster a sense of community.

Engage and Respond: When users share UGC, make an effort to engage with them. Like, comment, or share their content to show your appreciation and encourage further interaction. Respond to their comments and messages to maintain a personal connection and deepen the sense of community.

Collaborate with Creators: Identify creators or influencers within your audience who consistently produce high-quality content. Collaborate with them to co-create content or promote your brand. This not only leverages their creative abilities but also strengthens their loyalty and influence within your community.

Provide Recognition and Rewards: Acknowledge and reward exceptional UGC. Consider featuring the creators in your newsletters, social media posts, or even within your books. Offer exclusive perks, discounts, or early access to new releases as a token of appreciation for their contributions.

Leverage UGC for Marketing Campaigns: Integrate UGC into your marketing campaigns by using it in advertisements, promotional materials, or testimonials. UGC adds authenticity and social proof to your marketing efforts, as it showcases real experiences and testimonials from your audience.

Monitor and Engage: Regularly monitor social media platforms and other channels for UGC related to your brand. Engage with creators, comment on their posts, and participate in conversations around their content. This demonstrates your active involvement and builds stronger relationships with your audience.

Remember to always obtain proper permissions and give credit to the creators of UGC. Respecting their intellectual property rights and privacy is crucial. By leveraging UGC, you not only create a more engaging and interactive experience for your audience but also foster a sense of community and make them an integral part of your brand story.

CHAPTER 6: SOCIAL MEDIA ADVERTISING AND PROMOTION

Understanding the Basics of Social Media Advertising

Targeting and Reaching Your Ideal Audience

Maximizing ROI and Budget Optimization

Social Media Advertising And Promotion

Social media advertising and promotion can be powerful tools to increase your reach, boost brand visibility, and drive targeted traffic to your books or author platform. Here are some tips for effectively utilizing social media advertising and promotion:

Set Clear Objectives: Define your goals for social media advertising and promotion. Do you want to increase brand awareness, drive website traffic, boost book sales, or grow your email list? Setting clear objectives helps you tailor your ad campaigns and measure their effectiveness.

Identify Your Target Audience: Understand your target audience's demographics, interests, and online behavior. Use the targeting options provided by social media platforms to reach the right people. Narrow down your audience based on factors like age, location, interests, and purchasing behavior to ensure your ads are seen by the most relevant users.

Choose the Right Platforms: Select the social media platforms that align with your target audience and objectives. Facebook, Instagram, Twitter, LinkedIn, and Pinterest are popular options, but consider where your audience is most active and engaged. Each platform offers unique features and ad formats, so choose the ones that best suit your needs.

Create Compelling Ad Content: Develop engaging and visually appealing ad content that captures attention and encourages clicks. Use high-quality images, captivating headlines, and concise copy that clearly communicates the value proposition of your books. A/B test different ad variations to optimize performance.

Utilize Ad Targeting Options: Take advantage of the targeting options provided by social media platforms. Utilize demographics, interests, behaviors, and custom audience targeting to ensure your ads are shown to the most relevant audience. Refine your targeting based on the performance data you gather to improve campaign effectiveness.

Use Remarketing: Implement remarketing campaigns to target users who have already shown interest in your books or visited your website. By retargeting these users with tailored ads, you can reinforce your brand message and increase the likelihood of conversion.

Monitor and Optimize Performance: Regularly monitor the performance of your ad campaigns using the analytics provided by the social media platforms. Pay attention to metrics like impressions, clicks, click-through rates, conversions, and return on ad spend. Make data-driven decisions and optimize your campaigns based on insights gained.

Leverage Influencer Marketing: Collaborate with influencers or authors in your genre to promote your books or author brand. Influencers can help amplify your message to their engaged audience, providing social proof and credibility. Choose influencers whose values align with yours and who have an audience that matches your target market.

Run Contests and Giveaways: Use social media platforms to run contests or giveaways that encourage user engagement and promote your books. Require participants to like, share, or comment on your posts to enter the contest, helping to increase the visibility of your content and attract new followers.

Test and Iterate: Experiment with different ad formats, targeting options, and messaging to find what resonates best with your audience. Continuously test and iterate your ad campaigns to optimize performance and maximize your return on investment.

Remember to comply with the advertising policies and guidelines of each social media platform to ensure your ads are approved and compliant. Social media advertising and promotion can be an effective way to amplify your author brand and reach a wider audience, but it's important to approach it strategically and monitor performance to achieve the best results.

Understanding The Basics Of Social Media Advertising

Social media advertising is a paid promotional strategy that involves creating and running ads on various social media platforms to reach a specific target audience. It allows you to amplify your brand's message, increase visibility, and drive desired actions such as website visits, book sales, or lead generation. Here are some key components and concepts to understand when it comes to social media advertising:

Ad Formats: Social media platforms offer various ad formats, including image ads, video ads, carousel ads, story ads, and more. Each format has its own specifications and advantages, so choose the format that best suits your advertising goals and resonates with your target audience.

Targeting Options: Social media platforms provide targeting options that allow you to define the audience you want to reach. You can target based on demographics (age, location, gender), interests, behaviors, connections, and more. Utilize these targeting options to ensure your ads are shown to the right people.

Ad Bidding: Social media advertising typically operates on an auction-based system, where advertisers bid for ad placements. You can set your budget and bidding strategy, such as cost per click (CPC) or cost per thousand impressions (CPM). The bid amount, relevance, and quality of your ad influence its chances of being displayed.

Ad Placement: Social media platforms offer various ad placements within their interface. These can include newsfeeds, sidebars, stories, search results, and more. Consider the user experience and engagement patterns on each platform when selecting ad placements.

Ad Creative: The visual and textual components of your ad, including images, videos, headlines, and ad copy, collectively form the ad creative. Create compelling and attention-grabbing creatives that align with your brand and resonate with your target audience. Experiment with different variations to find what works best.

Call-to-Action (CTA): A CTA is a specific instruction or prompt that encourages users to take a desired action, such as "Shop Now," "Sign Up," or "Learn More." Incorporate a clear and persuasive CTA in your ad to guide users towards the action you want them to take.

Tracking and Analytics: Social media platforms provide analytics and tracking tools to measure the performance of your ads. Monitor metrics such as impressions, clicks, click-through rates (CTR), conversions, and return on ad spend (ROAS). Use these insights to optimize your campaigns and make data-driven decisions.

Remarketing: Remarketing allows you to target users who have previously interacted with your brand or visited your website. It helps you reconnect with interested users and increase the chances of conversion by showing them relevant ads as they browse social media platforms.

Ad Testing: Experiment with different ad variations to identify what performs best. Test different visuals, headlines, ad copies, and CTAs to optimize your campaigns. Split testing, also known as A/B testing, involves running multiple versions of an ad to compare their effectiveness and determine the winning variation.

Campaign Optimization: Continuously monitor and optimize your ad campaigns based on performance data. Adjust targeting, ad creative, budget, and bidding strategies to improve results and maximize your advertising ROI.

It's important to keep up with the evolving features and policies of social media platforms to make the most of your social media advertising efforts. Regularly review your ad performance, adapt your strategies, and stay informed about new advertising options and trends in the social media advertising world.

Targeting And Reaching Your Ideal Audience

Targeting and reaching your ideal audience is a crucial aspect of social media marketing. By effectively targeting your audience, you can ensure that your messages reach the right people who are most likely to be interested in your books. Here are some strategies to help you target and reach your ideal audience on social media:

Define Your Audience: Start by clearly defining your target audience. Consider demographics such as age, gender, location, and language. Additionally, think about their interests, preferences, and behaviors related to books, genres, and relevant topics. Develop detailed buyer personas to guide your targeting efforts.

Utilize Platform Targeting Options: Take advantage of the targeting options provided by social media platforms. Each platform offers different targeting capabilities to help you narrow down your audience. You can target based on demographics, interests, behaviors, connections, and more. Tailor your targeting to match your defined audience characteristics.

Lookalike Audiences: Social media platforms offer the option to create lookalike audiences. These audiences are generated based on the characteristics and behaviors of your existing audience or customer base. By creating lookalike audiences, you can reach new people who share similar traits and interests with your existing audience.

Retargeting: Implement retargeting campaigns to reach users

who have previously interacted with your brand or website. Set up tracking pixels or use email lists to create custom audiences that you can target with specific messaging. Retargeting helps keep your brand top of mind and increases the likelihood of conversion.

Interest-based Targeting: Leverage interest-based targeting to reach users who have shown a specific interest in books, authors, genres, or related topics. Many social media platforms provide interest categories that you can select to narrow down your audience based on their stated interests, online behavior, and engagements.

Custom Audiences: Utilize custom audiences to target specific groups of people. You can upload your own customer lists or email lists to create custom audiences. This allows you to directly target existing customers, subscribers, or fans and deliver tailored messaging to them.

Geographic Targeting: If you have a specific geographic focus, such as promoting a local book signing event or targeting readers in a particular region, make use of geographic targeting options. Specify the locations where you want your ads to be shown to ensure you reach the right audience within your desired area.

Use Audience Insights: Social media platforms often provide audience insights and analytics tools that can help you understand the demographics and interests of your current audience. Analyze these insights to gain a deeper understanding of your audience and refine your targeting strategy.

Test and Refine: Continuously test and refine your targeting parameters based on the performance data you gather. Monitor key metrics such as reach, engagement, click-through rates, and conversions. Experiment with different targeting options and variations to optimize your campaigns and reach your ideal audience more effectively.

Monitor and Adjust: Regularly monitor the performance of your campaigns and make adjustments as needed. Analyze the data and insights provided by social media platforms to identify trends, audience preferences, and areas for improvement. Adapt your targeting strategy based on the results to ensure you're reaching the right audience with the right message.

Remember that targeting is an ongoing process, and it's important to stay updated with your audience's preferences and behaviors. Regularly evaluate and refine your targeting strategy to reach your ideal audience and maximize the impact of your social media marketing efforts.

Maximizing Roi And Budget Optimization

Maximizing return on investment (ROI) and optimizing your budget are essential considerations when running social media advertising campaigns. Here are some tips to help you make the most of your budget and maximize ROI:

Set Clear Objectives: Clearly define your goals and objectives for your social media advertising campaigns. Whether it's driving book sales, increasing website traffic, or growing your email list, having specific objectives will guide your strategy and help you measure success.

Define Key Performance Indicators (KPIs): Determine the key metrics you'll use to measure the success of your campaigns. These may include metrics such as click-through rates, conversion rates, cost per acquisition, or return on ad spend. By tracking these KPIs, you can evaluate the effectiveness of your campaigns and make data-driven decisions.

Start with a Testing Phase: When starting a new campaign, allocate a portion of your budget to a testing phase. Test different ad formats, creatives, targeting options, and messaging variations to identify what resonates best with your audience. Use the data from these tests to inform your ongoing campaign optimization.

Monitor and Optimize: Regularly monitor the performance of your campaigns and make data-driven optimizations. Adjust your targeting parameters, creative elements, ad placements, and bidding strategies based on the insights you gather. Continuously test and refine your campaigns to improve their performance over time.

Focus on High-Quality Targeting: Refine your targeting to focus on the most relevant audience for your books. The more precise and targeted your audience, the higher the likelihood of engagement and conversion. Continuously analyze the performance of different targeting parameters to identify the most effective combinations.

Utilize Ad Scheduling: Consider the times and days when your audience is most active on social media. Use ad scheduling features provided by social media platforms to show your ads during peak engagement periods. This helps maximize the visibility and impact of your campaigns while minimizing wasted impressions.

Implement Conversion Tracking: Set up conversion tracking to measure the actions users take after interacting with your ads. This could include purchases, email sign-ups, or website form submissions. By tracking conversions, you can evaluate the effectiveness of your campaigns and optimize them for better results.

Implement Remarketing Campaigns: Implement remarketing campaigns to re-engage users who have previously interacted with your brand. Remarketing allows you to stay top of mind with potential customers and increase the likelihood of conversion. Customize your messaging and offers to resonate with these audiences.

Monitor Ad Frequency: Be mindful of ad frequency, which refers to the number of times a user sees your ad. High ad frequency can lead to ad fatigue and decreased engagement. Monitor frequency and adjust your campaign settings or creative rotations to prevent overexposure.

Test Different Ad Formats: Experiment with different ad formats to determine which ones yield the best results. Different formats can have varying levels of engagement and performance depending on your target audience and objectives. Test formats such as image ads, video ads, carousel ads, or interactive ads to find what works best for your campaigns.

Keep Up with Platform Updates and Features: Stay informed about updates and new features on social media platforms. These updates often provide new targeting options, ad formats, and optimization tools that can enhance your campaigns. Take advantage of these features to maximize your ROI.

By implementing these strategies, monitoring performance, and making data-driven optimizations, you can maximize your social media advertising budget and achieve a higher return on investment. Regularly assess your campaigns, adapt to changing trends and audience preferences, and allocate your budget to the strategies that yield the best results for your book marketing goals.

CHAPTER 7:
HARNESSING
THE POWER OF
INFLUENCER
MARKETING

Identifying and Collaborating with Influencers

Strategies for Authentic Partnerships

Measuring and Tracking Influencer Campaigns

Harnessing The Power Of Influencer Marketing

Influencer marketing is a powerful strategy that involves collaborating with influencers to promote your books or author brand to their engaged audience. Influencers have established credibility, a loyal following, and the ability to sway the opinions and behaviors of their followers. Here are some steps to harness the power of influencer marketing:

Identify Relevant Influencers: Research and identify influencers in your book's genre or niche who align with your brand values and target audience. Look for influencers who have an engaged and active following. Consider factors such as their reach, engagement rates, content quality, and relevance to your target market.

Build Relationships: Start building relationships with influencers by engaging with their content, sharing their posts, and commenting on their posts. Show genuine interest in their work and establish a connection before reaching out for potential collaborations. This helps create a foundation of trust and authenticity.

Define Collaboration Objectives: Clearly define your collaboration objectives. Do you want influencers to create sponsored content, share book reviews, host giveaways, or participate in author interviews? Determine the type of collaboration that aligns with your goals and offers value to both the influencer and their audience.

Outreach and Negotiation: Reach out to the influencers you've identified and express your interest in collaborating. Personalize your outreach and explain why you believe a collaboration would be beneficial. Discuss compensation, deliverables, and any guidelines or requirements. Be open to negotiation and find a mutually beneficial arrangement.

Authentic Integration: Encourage influencers to authentically integrate your books or brand into their content. Allow them creative freedom to present your offerings in a way that resonates with their audience. Influencers know their followers best, so trust their expertise in creating content that feels genuine and aligns with their usual style.

Track Performance: Set up tracking mechanisms to measure the performance of influencer collaborations. Track metrics such as engagement rates, website traffic, book sales, or social media follower growth. Use unique discount codes or affiliate links to attribute conversions to specific influencers. Analyze the data to evaluate the effectiveness of each collaboration.

Long-term Relationships: Consider developing long-term relationships with influencers who align well with your brand. Continuously collaborate with them on multiple campaigns to build familiarity and establish ongoing partnerships. Long-term collaborations can create a stronger connection with the influencer's audience and amplify the impact of your marketing efforts.

Disclosure and Compliance: Ensure compliance with relevant advertising guidelines and regulations. Influencer content that involves sponsored or paid partnerships should be clearly disclosed to maintain transparency with the audience. Familiarize yourself with the disclosure requirements in the countries where you and the influencers operate.

Micro-influencers and Nano-influencers: Consider working with micro-influencers and nano-influencers. These influencers typically have smaller but highly engaged and niche-specific audiences. Collaborating with them can result in more targeted reach, stronger connections, and higher engagement rates compared to larger-scale influencers.

Authenticity and Relationships: Cultivate authentic relationships with influencers. Show appreciation for their work, engage with their content, and support them beyond just collaboration requests. Building genuine relationships with influencers can lead to mutual support and a network of advocates who genuinely enjoy your books and are more likely to promote them authentically.

Influencer marketing can be a valuable addition to your social media strategy, as it allows you to tap into the existing influence and reach of trusted individuals in your industry. By leveraging their credibility and audience engagement, you can expand your brand's visibility, build trust, and connect with a wider audience of potential readers.

Identifying And Collaborating With Influencers

Identifying and collaborating with influencers requires careful research and consideration to ensure they are the right fit for your book marketing goals. Here are some steps to help you in the process:

Define Your Target Audience: Before you start searching for influencers, clearly define your target audience. Consider demographics, interests, and preferences of your ideal readers. Understanding your audience will help you identify influencers who have a relevant following.

Research Relevant Platforms: Determine which social media platforms are popular among your target audience. Platforms like Instagram, YouTube, TikTok, and Twitter are commonly used by influencers to engage with their followers. Focus your research on platforms where your audience is most active.

Look for Influencers in Your Genre or Niche: Search for influencers who specialize in your book's genre or niche. Look for those who have a genuine interest and expertise in your genre, as they are more likely to have an engaged following of readers who share similar interests.

Use Influencer Discovery Tools: Utilize influencer discovery tools to help you find relevant influencers. These tools allow you to search for influencers based on criteria such as location, follower count, engagement rate, and content type. Some popular influencer discovery tools include BuzzSumo, HypeAuditor, and Upfluence.

Explore Hashtags and Keywords: Search for relevant hashtags and keywords related to your genre or niche on social media platforms. Explore the content shared using those hashtags to identify influencers who are actively engaging with your target audience. Look for influencers who consistently produce high-quality content and have an engaged following.

Assess Influencer Authenticity and Engagement: It's important to evaluate an influencer's authenticity and engagement. Look for influencers who have genuine interactions with their followers, receive meaningful comments on their posts, and have an active community. Assess their content quality, relevance, and overall aesthetic to ensure it aligns with your brand.

Review Metrics and Analytics: Examine an influencer's metrics and analytics to gauge their reach and effectiveness. Look at metrics such as follower count, engagement rate, average likes and comments per post, and audience demographics. This data will give you insights into their audience's size and level of engagement.

Evaluate Influencer Relevance: Consider an influencer's relevance beyond just numbers. Look for influencers whose values align with your brand, and whose content demonstrates an understanding of and passion for your genre. Collaborating with influencers who genuinely appreciate your books will result in more authentic promotions.

Engage and Build Relationships: Once you've identified potential influencers, start engaging with their content. Like their posts, leave thoughtful comments, and share their content if it resonates with your audience. Building a relationship and demonstrating genuine interest in their work can increase the likelihood of successful collaborations.

Reach Out with a Personalized Proposal: When reaching out to influencers, personalize your approach. Explain why you believe a collaboration would be a good fit and highlight how it can benefit both parties. Be clear about your expectations, deliverables, and compensation. Customize your proposal to show that you've done your research and understand their audience and content style.

Negotiate and Establish Terms: If the influencer shows interest in collaborating, discuss and negotiate the terms of the collaboration. This may include the type and frequency of content, compensation, timelines, and any specific guidelines. Be open to negotiation and find a mutually beneficial agreement.

Monitor and Measure Results: Once the collaboration is live, track the performance of the influencer's content. Monitor engagement, website traffic, book sales, and other relevant metrics. Analyze the results to evaluate the success of the collaboration and make data-driven decisions for future collaborations.

Remember, the key to successful influencer collaborations is finding influencers who genuinely connect with your audience and align with your brand values. By taking the time to research, build relationships, and establish mutually beneficial collaborations, you can tap into the power of influencers to expand your book's reach and engage with new readers.

Strategies For Authentic Partnerships

Authentic partnerships with influencers are crucial for building trust, reaching a wider audience, and promoting your books effectively. Here are some strategies to foster authentic partnerships with influencers:

Align with Relevant Influencers: Choose influencers who align with your brand values, target audience, and book genre. Look for influencers who genuinely appreciate and engage with content similar to yours. This alignment will ensure that their audience is more likely to be interested in your books.

Engage with Influencers Organically: Before reaching out for collaboration, engage with influencers' content organically. Like, comment, and share their posts to show genuine interest and support. This establishes a foundation for building a relationship and increases the chances of them being open to working with you.

Personalize Your Outreach: When reaching out to influencers, personalize your messages and proposals. Reference specific content they have created that resonated with you, and explain why you believe a collaboration would be a good fit. Tailor your approach to show that you've done your research and are genuinely interested in working with them.

Offer Value to Influencers: Provide influencers with something valuable in exchange for their promotion. This could include advanced copies of your book, exclusive content, access to events, or special discounts for their audience. Show that you appreciate their contribution and are committed to creating a mutually beneficial partnership.

Be Transparent and Authentic: Maintain transparency throughout your collaboration. Clearly communicate your expectations, goals, and any guidelines or requirements. Allow influencers creative freedom to craft their content in a way that resonates with their audience, while also ensuring it aligns with your brand values.

Collaborate on Meaningful Content: Work with influencers to create meaningful and engaging content that showcases your books in an authentic way. Encourage them to share their honest opinions, personal experiences, or creative interpretations of your books. This authenticity will resonate with their audience and build trust.

Encourage Honest Reviews: Request honest reviews from influencers, allowing them the freedom to express their genuine opinions about your books. Authentic reviews carry more weight and can influence their audience's purchasing decisions. Embrace constructive feedback and use it to improve your future work.

Foster Long-Term Relationships: Look beyond one-time collaborations and aim to build long-term relationships with influencers. Continuously engage with them, support their work, and explore opportunities for ongoing partnerships. Long-term relationships allow for deeper connections and more authentic promotions.

Share Influencer Content: Once influencers create content promoting your books, share it on your own social media platforms or website. This not only shows appreciation for their efforts but also extends the reach of their content and exposes their audience to your brand.

Measure and Acknowledge Results: Monitor the performance of influencer collaborations by tracking metrics such as engagement, website traffic, book sales, and follower growth. Acknowledge the impact the influencer had on your book's success and publicly thank them for their support. This shows gratitude and encourages continued collaboration.

Maintain Open Communication: Keep the lines of communication open with influencers throughout the collaboration process. Be responsive, provide any necessary support, and address any concerns or questions they may have. Building a strong working relationship based on open communication is key to successful partnerships.

Remember, authentic partnerships are built on trust, shared values, and genuine connections. By nurturing relationships with influencers and approaching collaborations with integrity and transparency, you can create impactful and authentic promotions for your books.

Measuring And Tracking Influencer Campaigns

Measuring and tracking the effectiveness of your influencer campaigns is crucial to understand their impact on your book marketing efforts. Here are some key steps to help you measure and track the success of your influencer campaigns:

Set Clear Goals and Objectives: Before launching an influencer campaign, define clear goals and objectives. These could include increasing book sales, driving website traffic, generating leads, growing social media following, or increasing brand awareness. Setting specific and measurable goals will provide a benchmark for evaluating the success of your campaign.

Use Unique URLs or Tracking Links: Provide influencers with unique URLs or tracking links to include in their content. These links should direct their audience to a specific landing page or trackable website page. By using unique links, you can attribute traffic and conversions directly to each influencer and measure their individual impact.

Implement UTM Parameters: UTM (Urchin Tracking Module) parameters are tags added to URLs that allow you to track the source, medium, and campaign associated with website traffic. Create unique UTM parameters for each influencer campaign and ensure that influencers use them when sharing links. This will help you track the traffic and conversions driven by each influencer.

Track Engagement Metrics: Monitor engagement metrics on the influencer's posts, such as likes, comments, shares, and saves. High engagement rates indicate that the influencer's audience is actively interacting with the content. Compare engagement rates across different influencers to identify which collaborations resonate most with your target audience.

Measure Website Traffic: Use web analytics tools like Google Analytics to track the amount of traffic driven to your website from influencer campaigns. Look for increases in overall website traffic and specific page views related to your book or landing pages. Analyze the data to identify which influencers are driving the most traffic and engagement.

Monitor Conversion Metrics: Measure the conversion metrics associated with your influencer campaigns. This could include book sales, newsletter sign-ups, ebook downloads, or any other desired action on your website. Set up conversion tracking pixels or codes to attribute these actions to specific influencers or campaigns. This data will help you determine the ROI of your influencer collaborations.

Monitor Social Media Metrics: Keep an eye on your social media metrics, such as follower growth, reach, impressions, and engagement on your own social media platforms. Compare these metrics during and after influencer collaborations to identify any spikes or changes in audience engagement and following.

Survey and Feedback: Consider surveying your audience to gather feedback on their experience with influencer campaigns. Ask questions about how they discovered your books, whether they made a purchase, and their overall satisfaction. Collecting feedback directly from your audience provides valuable insights into the impact and effectiveness of influencer collaborations.

Analyze Sales Data: Monitor your book sales data during and after influencer campaigns. Compare sales during the campaign period to the baseline sales to identify any increases or changes. Track sales by different influencers or campaigns to assess their individual contribution.

Calculate ROI: Calculate the return on investment (ROI) for each influencer campaign. Compare the revenue generated from book sales or other conversions against the costs associated with collaborating with the influencer (e.g., compensation, product samples). This analysis will help you determine which collaborations provide the best return on investment.

Track Brand Mentions and Sentiment: Monitor social media and online platforms for brand mentions and sentiment related to your influencer campaigns. Analyze the sentiment of these mentions (positive, negative, or neutral) to gauge the overall perception of your brand. This qualitative data can provide insights into the effectiveness of influencer collaborations beyond just the quantitative metrics.

Evaluate Influencer Feedback: Communicate with the influencers post-campaign to gather their feedback on the collaboration process, audience response, and any insights they gained. Their input can help you improve future influencer campaigns and build stronger relationships with influencers.

By combining these measurement techniques, you can gain a comprehensive understanding of the impact and effectiveness of your influencer campaigns. Use the insights gained to optimize your future collaborations and allocate resources towards influencers who drive the most meaningful results for your book marketing efforts.

CHAPTER 8:
ANALYTICS AND
PERFORMANCE
TRACKING

Essential Social Media Metrics to Monitor

Tools and Techniques for Analytics

Adapting Strategies Based on Insights

Analytics And Performance Tracking

Analytics and performance tracking play a crucial role in evaluating the success of your social media efforts and informing your future strategies. Here are some key aspects of analytics and performance tracking for social media:

Set Clear Objectives: Start by defining clear objectives for your social media efforts. These objectives could include increasing brand awareness, driving website traffic, generating leads, boosting engagement, or increasing conversions. Clearly defined objectives will guide your analytics efforts and help you measure the right metrics.

Utilize Social Media Analytics Tools: Most social media platforms provide built-in analytics tools that offer insights into your performance. Facebook Insights, Twitter Analytics, Instagram Insights, and LinkedIn Analytics are examples of platform-specific analytics tools. These tools provide data on audience demographics, engagement metrics, reach, impressions, and more.

Use Website Analytics Tools: Integrate your social media channels with website analytics tools like Google Analytics. This will help you track social media-driven traffic, conversions, bounce rates, and other website metrics. Use UTM parameters and tracking codes to attribute website traffic and conversions to specific social media campaigns or posts.

Measure Reach and Impressions: Reach and impressions are key metrics that indicate the visibility and exposure of your social media content. Reach refers to the number of unique users who have seen your content, while impressions represent the total number of times your content has been viewed. Monitor these metrics to assess your content's overall visibility and potential audience reach.

Track Engagement Metrics: Engagement metrics, such as likes, comments, shares, and retweets, provide insights into how well your content resonates with your audience. Analyze these metrics to understand which types of content generate higher engagement and adjust your content strategy accordingly. Engagement metrics also help gauge the level of interaction and interest from your audience.

Monitor Follower Growth: Keep an eye on your follower growth rate to understand how effectively you are attracting and retaining an audience on each social media platform. A steady increase in followers indicates a healthy and engaged community. Analyze follower growth alongside your content and campaigns to identify any correlation.

Analyze Audience Demographics: Social media analytics tools provide demographic data about your audience, including age, gender, location, and interests. Understanding your audience's demographics can help you tailor your content, campaigns, and messaging to better resonate with their preferences and needs.

Assess Referral Traffic: Use website analytics tools to track the amount of traffic driven to your website from social media platforms. Analyze the performance of different social media channels and specific posts to identify which channels and content are driving the most traffic. This data can help you optimize your content and promotional strategies.

Measure Conversions and Goals: Define conversion goals, such as newsletter sign-ups, ebook downloads, or product purchases, and track them using website analytics tools. Set up conversion tracking to attribute conversions to specific social media channels or campaigns. This data helps you evaluate the impact of your social media efforts on driving desired actions.

Monitor Sentiment and Brand Mentions: Keep an eye on social media mentions of your brand or book titles to understand the sentiment and perception surrounding your brand. Utilize social listening tools to track brand mentions and sentiment in real-time. This data helps you gauge the overall sentiment, identify potential issues, and engage with your audience proactively.

Track Competitor Performance: Monitor your competitors' social media presence and performance to gain insights and benchmark your own performance. Analyze their content strategies, engagement levels, follower growth, and audience demographics to identify opportunities for improvement and differentiation.

Regularly Review and Adjust: Continuously review your analytics data to identify trends, patterns, and areas for improvement. Use the insights gained to refine your social media strategy, optimize content, and allocate resources effectively. Regularly adjust your tactics based on the analytics data to maximize your social media performance.

Remember, analytics and performance tracking provide valuable insights into the effectiveness of your social media efforts. Use the data to measure your progress, identify areas of success, and make informed decisions to optimize your social media strategy.

Essential Social Media Metrics To Monitor

Monitoring social media metrics is essential to understand the performance and impact of your social media efforts. Here are some key social media metrics that you should monitor:

Reach: Reach measures the number of unique users who have seen your social media content. It indicates the potential audience size that your content has reached. Monitoring reach helps you understand the visibility of your content and assess your overall audience reach.

Impressions: Impressions represent the total number of times your social media content has been viewed. Unlike reach, impressions count multiple views by the same user. Monitoring impressions helps you understand the total exposure and frequency of your content.

Engagement Rate: Engagement rate measures the level of interaction and engagement your content receives from your audience. It is typically calculated as the total engagements (likes, comments, shares, etc.) divided by the total reach or impressions, multiplied by 100 to get a percentage. Monitoring engagement rate helps you gauge the effectiveness of your content in capturing audience attention and driving interaction.

Follower Growth: Follower growth tracks the increase or decrease in the number of followers on your social media accounts over time. Monitoring follower growth helps you assess the effectiveness of your content, campaigns, and overall social media strategy in attracting and retaining an audience.

Click-through Rate (CTR): CTR measures the percentage of users who click on a link or call-to-action in your social media posts. It indicates the effectiveness of your content in driving traffic to your website or landing pages. Monitoring CTR helps you assess the performance of your call-to-action and the effectiveness of your content in generating clicks.

Conversion Rate: Conversion rate measures the percentage of users who complete a desired action, such as making a purchase, signing up for a newsletter, or downloading an ebook. It helps you understand the effectiveness of your social media campaigns in driving desired outcomes. Monitoring conversion rate allows you to assess the ROI of your social media efforts.

Referral Traffic: Referral traffic tracks the amount of traffic driven to your website from social media platforms. It helps you understand which social media channels and specific posts are driving the most traffic. Monitoring referral traffic allows you to optimize your content and promotional strategies.

Sentiment Analysis: Sentiment analysis measures the sentiment or emotional tone associated with social media mentions of your brand or book titles. It helps you gauge the overall sentiment surrounding your brand and understand the perception of your audience. Monitoring sentiment analysis allows you to proactively address any negative sentiment or engage with your audience based on their sentiment.

Audience Demographics: Understanding the demographics of your social media audience is crucial for tailoring your content and campaigns to their preferences and needs. Monitor audience demographics such as age, gender, location, and interests to ensure you are reaching and engaging the right target audience.

Share of Voice: Share of voice measures the percentage of conversations or mentions related to your brand compared to your competitors within a specific industry or topic. It helps you assess your brand's visibility and impact relative to competitors. Monitoring share of voice allows you to identify areas where you can increase your brand's presence and engagement.

Remember, these metrics should be aligned with your social media goals and objectives. Regularly monitoring and analyzing these metrics will provide insights into the performance and effectiveness of your social media strategy, allowing you to make data-driven decisions and optimizations.

Tools And Techniques For Analytics

There are various tools and techniques available to help you analyze and track social media analytics effectively. Here are some commonly used tools and techniques for social media analytics:

Native Analytics Platforms: Most social media platforms provide built-in analytics tools that offer insights into your account's performance. Facebook Insights, Twitter Analytics, Instagram Insights, LinkedIn Analytics, and YouTube Analytics are examples of native analytics platforms. These tools provide data on audience demographics, engagement metrics, reach, impressions, and more specific to each platform.

Google Analytics: Google Analytics is a powerful web analytics tool that helps you track and measure website traffic, conversions, and user behavior. By integrating Google Analytics with your social media channels, you can track social media-driven traffic, conversions, and other website metrics. It allows you to set up goals, track conversions, create custom reports, and gain in-depth insights into the performance of your social media campaigns.

Social Media Management Tools: Social media management tools like Hootsuite, Buffer, Sprout Social, and Later offer analytics features that consolidate data from multiple social media platforms. These tools provide a centralized dashboard where you can monitor and analyze key metrics across different channels, schedule posts, and generate reports.

URL Shorteners and UTM Parameters: URL shorteners like Bitly and Rebrandly can help you track the performance of specific links shared on social media. By shortening URLs and adding UTM parameters, you can create trackable links that provide detailed analytics on clicks, traffic sources, and conversions. UTM parameters allow you to attribute traffic and conversions to specific social media campaigns, posts, or influencers.

Social Listening Tools: Social listening tools like Mention, Brandwatch, and Sprout Social enable you to monitor social media conversations and track brand mentions, sentiment, and trends. These tools help you understand how your brand or book titles are being discussed across social media platforms, identify emerging trends, and gain insights into audience sentiment.

Influencer Marketing Platforms: If you are running influencer campaigns, utilizing influencer marketing platforms like Upfluence, Traackr, or AspireIQ can provide analytics and performance tracking features. These platforms offer data on influencer reach, engagement, audience demographics, and the effectiveness of influencer collaborations.

Custom Dashboards and Reports: Creating custom dashboards and reports using tools like Google Data Studio or Microsoft Excel can help you visualize and analyze your social media data. These tools allow you to combine data from multiple sources, create interactive visualizations, and customize reports according to your specific needs.

A/B Testing: A/B testing involves creating different variations of your social media content or campaigns and comparing their performance. By testing different elements such as headlines, images, calls-to-action, or posting times, you can identify which variations resonate better with your audience and generate higher engagement or conversions.

Surveys and Feedback: In addition to analytics tools, collecting feedback directly from your audience through surveys or social media polls can provide valuable insights. Surveys can help you understand audience preferences, satisfaction, and the impact of your social media efforts on their perception and actions.

By utilizing these tools and techniques, you can gather and analyze data, track key metrics, and gain actionable insights to optimize your social media strategy and improve your book marketing efforts. It's important to select the tools and techniques that align with your specific goals, budget, and analytics requirements.

Adapting Strategies Based On Insights

Adapting your social media strategies based on insights is crucial for optimizing your approach and achieving better results. Here are some steps to effectively adapt your strategies based on the insights you gather:

Regularly Review and Analyze Data: Continuously monitor and analyze the data from your social media analytics tools. Look for trends, patterns, and key performance indicators that align with your goals. Identify areas of success and areas that need improvement.

Identify Top-performing Content: Determine which types of content resonate best with your audience by analyzing engagement metrics such as likes, comments, shares, and clicks. Identify the common characteristics of your top-performing content, such as topic, format, style, or visuals. This will help you understand what content to prioritize and produce more of in the future.

Optimize Posting Times and Frequency: Analyze the data on when your audience is most active and engaged on each social media platform. Adjust your posting schedule to align with these peak times. Experiment with different posting frequencies and observe the impact on engagement. Continuously monitor and adapt your posting times and frequency based on the insights you gather.

Refine Targeting and Audience Segmentation: Analyze the demographic data available from your social media analytics tools to understand your audience better. Identify any new or untapped audience segments that are showing interest in your content. Use this information to refine your targeting and create more personalized and relevant content for different audience segments.

Experiment with Different Formats and Channels: Don't be afraid to try new content formats, such as videos, infographics, or live streams, to diversify your content strategy. Experiment with different social media channels and evaluate their performance. If a particular format or channel performs well, consider incorporating it into your regular content strategy.

Test and Optimize Ad Campaigns: If you're running social media advertising campaigns, regularly review the performance data and optimize your campaigns based on the insights you gather. Test different ad variations, targeting options, and messaging to identify what works best for your audience. Allocate your ad budget towards the campaigns that yield the highest ROI.

Engage with Your Audience: Pay attention to the comments, messages, and mentions you receive on social media. Respond to questions, address concerns, and engage in conversations with your audience. This not only helps build a stronger connection with your audience but also provides valuable insights into their preferences and needs.

Stay Updated with Social Media Trends: Stay abreast of the latest social media trends, algorithm changes, and platform updates. Follow industry influencers, join relevant communities, and participate in social media discussions. Adapt your strategies to leverage these trends and changes to your advantage.

Set Goals and Track Progress: Continuously set clear and

measurable goals for your social media efforts. Regularly track your progress towards these goals using the metrics and analytics data available to you. This will help you understand the impact of your adaptations and ensure you are on track to achieve your objectives.

Remember, adaptation is an ongoing process. Social media platforms and audience preferences are constantly evolving, so it's important to regularly evaluate your strategies, make data-driven adjustments, and stay agile in your approach. By leveraging insights and adapting your strategies accordingly, you can optimize your social media presence and drive better results for your book marketing efforts.

CHAPTER 9: MANAGING CHALLENGES AND HANDLING ONLINE CRITICISM

Dealing with Negative Feedback and Trolls

Strategies for Managing Online Reputation

Turning Criticism into Opportunities for Growth

Managing Challenges And Handling Online Criticism

Managing challenges and handling online criticism is an important aspect of maintaining a positive online presence. Here are some strategies to help you effectively deal with challenges and criticism on social media:

Stay Calm and Professional: When faced with criticism or challenges, it's essential to remain calm and composed. Responding in a professional manner shows that you take feedback seriously and are open to resolving any issues. Avoid responding defensively or engaging in arguments, as it can escalate the situation further.

Assess the Validity of the Criticism: Take the time to evaluate the criticism objectively. Determine if it has any merit and if there are any areas where you can improve. Constructive feedback can provide valuable insights for growth and help you better understand your audience's needs and preferences.

Respond Promptly and Thoughtfully: Timely responses demonstrate your commitment to addressing concerns. Craft thoughtful responses that acknowledge the feedback and provide appropriate information or solutions. Even if you can't fully resolve the issue publicly, offer to continue the conversation privately through direct messages or email.

Address Concerns with Empathy: Show empathy and understanding towards the concerns raised by your audience. Acknowledge their perspective and let them know that you value their feedback. Offer sincere apologies if necessary and assure them that you will take their concerns into consideration.

Take the Conversation Offline: If the criticism or challenge requires a more in-depth discussion or resolution, consider taking it offline. Provide contact information or direct the person to a customer support channel where they can receive personalized assistance. This helps maintain privacy and allows for a more focused and effective resolution.

Monitor and Manage Online Conversations: Regularly monitor your social media channels for any potential challenges or criticism. Respond promptly to inquiries, comments, and messages. Use social listening tools to keep track of mentions of your brand or book titles and address any concerns or negative sentiment proactively.

Engage with Positive Comments and Reviews: While it's important to address criticism, don't forget to engage with positive comments and reviews as well. Responding to positive feedback shows appreciation and encourages continued support from your audience. It helps create a balanced and positive online presence.

Learn from Feedback: View criticism as an opportunity for growth and improvement. Use it as a chance to evaluate your strategies, content, or customer experience. Adapt and make necessary changes based on the feedback received, demonstrating your commitment to providing the best experience for your audience.

Develop a Crisis Management Plan: Prepare for potential crises by developing a crisis management plan. Anticipate possible scenarios and outline steps to address them. Identify key stakeholders, establish communication protocols, and designate team members responsible for handling crises. Being prepared can help you respond effectively and mitigate the impact of any challenges or negative situations.

Seek Support from Your Community: Engage with your loyal supporters and community members during challenging times. They can provide encouragement, defend your brand when necessary, and help counteract any negativity. Foster a positive and supportive online community that rallies behind your brand.

Remember, not all criticism is valid or worth responding to. Evaluate the intention and relevance of the feedback before engaging. Prioritize constructive feedback that can help you improve and make necessary adjustments to your strategies. Maintaining a respectful and professional approach, even in challenging situations, will help you build trust and credibility with your audience.

Dealing With Negative Feedback And Trolls

Dealing with negative feedback and trolls on social media can be challenging, but it's important to handle them effectively to maintain a positive online presence. Here are some strategies to help you deal with negative feedback and trolls:

Assess the Situation: Take a moment to assess the nature of the feedback or comment. Determine if it is genuine criticism or simply an attempt to provoke or cause harm. Understanding the intention behind the negativity can help you determine the best course of action.

Stay Calm and Don't Take it Personally: It's natural to feel defensive or upset when faced with negative feedback or trolling. However, it's important to remain calm and avoid taking it personally. Remember that not all criticism is valid, and trolls are often seeking attention or trying to provoke a reaction.

Don't Engage in Arguments: Engaging in arguments or responding emotionally to trolls can fuel the negativity and escalate the situation. Instead, choose your battles wisely and avoid getting into a back-and-forth exchange. Responding calmly and professionally is more likely to defuse the situation.

Focus on Constructive Feedback: Differentiate between genuine constructive feedback and baseless negativity. Constructive criticism can provide valuable insights for improvement. Respond to constructive feedback with gratitude and show your willingness to address the concerns raised.

Use Humor or Ignore: Sometimes, using humor to respond to trolls can diffuse the situation and show that you're not taking their negativity seriously. However, if the comment or behavior is extreme, offensive, or violates the platform's guidelines, it may be best to ignore and report it. Blocking or muting the individual can also prevent further interactions.

Encourage Positive Dialogue: Encourage positive dialogue and engagement by highlighting the importance of respectful communication. Lead by example and respond to positive comments or questions from your audience. This helps shift the focus to constructive conversations and encourages others to do the same.

Moderate Comments and User-generated Content: Implement moderation measures to filter out offensive or inappropriate comments on your social media platforms. Set clear community guidelines and make them visible to your audience. This helps create a safe and respectful environment for discussions.

Seek Support from Your Community: Engage with your loyal supporters and community members during challenging times. They can provide encouragement, defend your brand when necessary, and help counteract any negativity. Building a strong and supportive community can act as a protective shield against trolls and negative feedback.

Report Abuse and Harassment: If you encounter online harassment or abusive behavior, report it to the social media platform. Most platforms have reporting mechanisms in place to address such issues. Provide specific details and evidence to support your report. By reporting abusive behavior, you contribute to maintaining a safer online environment.

Focus on the Positive: Don't let negative feedback or trolls overshadow the positive aspects of your online presence. Focus on the support and appreciation you receive from your audience. Surround yourself with positivity and remember that trolls and negativity are a small fraction of your overall audience.

It's important to remember that you cannot control the actions or opinions of others, but you have control over how you respond and manage the situation. By staying calm, maintaining professionalism, and focusing on constructive engagement, you can effectively handle negative feedback and minimize the impact of trolls on your online presence.

Strategies For Managing Online Reputation

Managing your online reputation is crucial for building a positive and credible image. Here are some strategies to help you effectively manage your online reputation:

Monitor Your Online Presence: Regularly monitor your online presence by conducting searches of your name, book titles, and relevant keywords. Set up Google Alerts or use online reputation management tools to receive notifications whenever your name or brand is mentioned online. This allows you to stay informed and address any issues promptly.

Respond Promptly and Professionally: When you come across any mentions or reviews, whether positive or negative, respond promptly and professionally. Acknowledge positive feedback with gratitude and engage in a genuine conversation. For negative feedback or complaints, address them calmly, offer solutions or explanations, and strive to resolve the issue to the best of your ability.

Encourage and Collect Positive Reviews: Actively encourage satisfied readers and fans to leave positive reviews on platforms such as Goodreads, Amazon, or other relevant book review sites. Positive reviews not only boost your reputation but also counterbalance any negative feedback that may arise.

Engage with Your Audience: Regularly engage with your audience on social media and other online platforms. Respond to comments, questions, and messages in a timely manner. Engaging with your audience shows that you value their input and helps build a positive relationship with them.

Build a Strong Online Brand: Consistently present yourself and your work in a positive and professional manner. Develop a strong brand identity that reflects your values and resonates with your target audience. Be authentic, transparent, and consistent in your messaging across all online platforms.

Publish High-Quality Content: Continuously produce and share high-quality content that showcases your expertise and provides value to your audience. Whether it's blog articles, social media posts, videos, or podcasts, focus on delivering content that educates, entertains, or inspires your readers. Valuable content contributes to a positive reputation and establishes you as a trusted authority in your field.

Be Mindful of Online Behavior: Practice good online etiquette and be mindful of how your actions may be perceived by others. Avoid engaging in controversial or offensive discussions, and refrain from participating in online arguments or heated debates. Maintain a professional and respectful tone in all your online interactions.

Address Negative Feedback Professionally: When faced with negative feedback, handle it professionally and constructively. Avoid responding defensively or engaging in arguments. Instead, take the opportunity to understand the concerns, address them calmly, and offer solutions or explanations. Handling negative feedback gracefully can demonstrate your commitment to customer satisfaction and reputation management.

Collaborate with Influencers and Thought Leaders: Partnering with influencers or thought leaders in your industry can help enhance your online reputation. Collaborate on projects, guest blog on their platforms, or engage in joint social media campaigns. Associating yourself with reputable individuals can positively impact how you are perceived online.

Continuously Learn and Improve: Stay updated with industry trends, feedback from your audience, and changes in online platforms. Continuously learn from your experiences and adapt your strategies accordingly. Be open to feedback and use it as an opportunity for growth and improvement.

Remember that building a positive online reputation takes time and effort. Consistency, professionalism, and a genuine commitment to providing value to your audience are key. By actively managing your online reputation, you can cultivate a positive image, build trust, and enhance your overall online presence.

Turning Criticism Into Opportunities For Growth

Criticism, when approached with the right mindset, can be valuable feedback that helps you grow and improve. Here are some strategies to turn criticism into opportunities for growth:

Be Open to Feedback: Embrace a growth mindset and be open to receiving feedback, even if it's negative. Understand that criticism can provide valuable insights and perspectives that you may have overlooked. Approach feedback with a willingness to learn and improve.

Separate Emotion from Evaluation: When receiving criticism, it's natural to have an emotional reaction. However, try to separate the emotional response from the evaluation itself. Take a step back, objectively assess the feedback, and focus on the constructive aspects.

Listen and Understand: Actively listen to the feedback and seek to understand the perspective of the person providing it. Ask clarifying questions to gain a deeper understanding of their concerns. This demonstrates your willingness to engage in a constructive dialogue.

Find the Grain of Truth: Look for the grain of truth in the criticism. Even if the feedback is delivered in a harsh manner, there may be a valid point hidden within it. Identify areas where you can make improvements or adjustments based on the feedback received.

Reflect and Self-Evaluate: Take the time to reflect on the

feedback and self-evaluate. Consider whether the criticism aligns with your goals, values, or desired outcomes. Assess whether there are areas where you can enhance your skills, knowledge, or approach.

Seek Different Perspectives: Seek out multiple perspectives on the criticism. Consult with trusted colleagues, mentors, or industry professionals who can provide objective insights. They may offer alternative viewpoints or solutions that can help you address the criticism effectively.

Take Action and Make Improvements: Use the feedback as a catalyst for growth and improvement. Develop an action plan to address the specific areas highlighted in the criticism. Implement changes, try new approaches, and track your progress over time.

Communicate and Show Progress: If appropriate, communicate with the person who provided the criticism and share how you have taken their feedback into account. Let them know about the improvements you have made or the steps you are taking to address their concerns. This demonstrates your commitment to growth and customer satisfaction.

Learn from Mistakes: Criticism often stems from mistakes or missteps. Treat these moments as valuable learning opportunities. Analyze what went wrong, understand the underlying causes, and develop strategies to prevent similar issues in the future.

Embrace Continuous Improvement: Adopt a mindset of continuous improvement. See every criticism as an opportunity to refine your skills, knowledge, and offerings. Continuously seek feedback, evaluate your performance, and make adjustments as needed. This mindset will help you stay adaptable and resilient in the face of criticism.

Remember, turning criticism into growth opportunities requires humility, self-reflection, and a commitment to personal and professional development. By embracing feedback, making improvements, and continuously learning, you can transform criticism into a catalyst for growth and success.

CHAPTER 10: BEYOND SOCIAL MEDIA: INTEGRATING OFFLINE AND ONLINE MARKETING

Integrating Traditional Marketing with Social Media Efforts

Leveraging Events and Book Launches

Building a Holistic Book Marketing Strategy

Beyond Social Media: Integrating Offline And Online Marketing

Integrating offline and online marketing strategies can help you reach a wider audience and create a cohesive brand experience. Here are some ways to go beyond social media and effectively integrate offline and online marketing:

Use Consistent Branding: Ensure that your branding elements, such as your logo, color palette, and messaging, are consistent across both offline and online channels. This consistency helps create a recognizable and cohesive brand image.

Include Online Information in Offline Collateral: Include your website URL, social media handles, and other online contact information on your offline marketing materials such as business cards, brochures, posters, and flyers. This encourages people to connect with you online and explore more about your brand.

Host Events and Workshops: Organize offline events and workshops related to your book or industry. Promote these events through social media, email marketing, and online platforms. Use online registration forms or ticketing systems to track attendance and capture leads.

Create Cross-Promotional Campaigns: Collaborate with offline businesses or influencers that share a similar target audience. Develop cross-promotional campaigns where you promote each other's products or services both online and offline. This allows you to tap into new networks and reach a wider audience.

Capture User-Generated Content Offline: Encourage attendees at your events or workshops to share their experiences on social media using event-specific hashtags or by tagging your brand. Display these user-generated posts on screens or walls at the event venue to create social proof and encourage online engagement.

Leverage Print Advertising: Consider using print advertising in newspapers, magazines, or local publications to reach a broader audience. Include a clear call-to-action that directs readers to your website or social media channels for more information or to make a purchase.

Utilize Direct Mail Campaigns: Send targeted direct mail campaigns to specific segments of your audience. Include personalized URLs (PURLs) or QR codes that direct recipients to specific landing pages or online offers. This helps track the effectiveness of your offline marketing efforts.

Engage with Local Communities: Participate in local community events, book fairs, or speaking engagements. Use these opportunities to connect with your target audience, share your expertise, and promote your online presence. Collect email addresses or social media follows to continue engaging with attendees after the event.

Offline-to-Online Contests and Giveaways: Run contests or giveaways at offline events where participants can enter by engaging with your online platforms. For example, they can enter by following your social media accounts or subscribing to your newsletter. This helps grow your online presence while providing an incentive for offline engagement.

Measure and Track Results: Use analytics tools to measure the effectiveness of your offline and online marketing efforts. Track website traffic, social media engagement, and conversions to determine which channels and strategies are generating the best results. This data will guide your future marketing decisions and help optimize your campaigns.

By integrating offline and online marketing strategies, you create a holistic approach that maximizes your reach and impact. The key is to maintain consistent branding, provide opportunities for offline and online interaction, and measure the effectiveness of your efforts to continually refine your marketing strategies.

Integrating Traditional Marketing With Social Media Efforts

Integrating traditional marketing with social media efforts can amplify your reach and create a cohesive brand experience across channels. Here are some ways to integrate traditional marketing with social media:

Include Social Media Icons in Print Materials: Add social media icons and handles to your print materials such as brochures, flyers, business cards, and posters. This encourages offline audiences to connect with you online and follow your social media profiles for updates and engagement.

Incorporate Social Media into Ad Campaigns: Include your social media handles and hashtags in traditional advertising channels such as TV commercials, radio spots, billboards, or print ads. Encourage viewers or listeners to engage with you on social media for exclusive content, promotions, or contests.

Leverage QR Codes: Place QR codes on your print materials or advertisements that link directly to your social media profiles or specific online promotions. This allows people to scan the code with their smartphones and easily connect with you on social media.

Run Social Media Contests with Offline Prizes: Host contests or giveaways on social media platforms, but offer offline prizes such as branded merchandise, signed copies of your book, or exclusive event tickets. Promote these contests through traditional marketing channels to attract both online and offline audiences.

Showcase User-Generated Content Offline: Select user-generated content from your social media platforms and feature it in your traditional marketing materials. For example, include customer testimonials or social media posts in your print ads or brochures to build social proof and encourage offline audiences to engage with you online.

Offline Events with Social Media Integration: Organize offline events such as book signings, workshops, or speaking engagements and promote them through your social media channels. Create event-specific hashtags and encourage attendees to share their experiences on social media. Display live social media feeds or posts during the event to encourage online engagement.

Use Social Media to Extend the Reach of Traditional PR: If you receive media coverage through traditional PR efforts, leverage social media to amplify the exposure. Share links to articles, interviews, or reviews on your social media platforms and encourage followers to engage with and share the content.

Cross-Promote Online and Offline Channels: Promote your traditional marketing efforts through your social media platforms and vice versa. For example, use social media to build anticipation for an upcoming TV or radio interview, or use your print ads to direct people to your social media platforms for behind-the-scenes content or exclusive offers.

Monitor and Engage with Traditional Media Mentions: Keep an eye on traditional media mentions such as newspaper articles, magazine features, or TV segments. Engage with these mentions by sharing them on your social media platforms, thanking the media outlets, and encouraging your followers to check out the coverage.

Measure and Analyze Results: Use tracking mechanisms, such as unique URLs or promo codes, to measure the impact of your traditional marketing efforts on social media engagement and conversions. Monitor the performance of different channels and campaigns to understand which strategies are most effective in driving online engagement.

Integrating traditional marketing with social media efforts allows you to leverage the strengths of each channel and create a seamless brand experience. By incorporating social media into your offline marketing strategies and vice versa, you can expand your reach, engage with a broader audience, and drive both online and offline interactions.

Leveraging Events And Book Launches

Events and book launches present excellent opportunities to generate excitement, engage with your audience, and promote your book. Here are some strategies for leveraging events and book launches:

Plan Ahead: Start planning your event or book launch well in advance to ensure a smooth and successful execution. Consider the venue, date, and logistics that align with your target audience and book theme.

Create Buzz: Generate anticipation and build excitement leading up to the event. Utilize your social media platforms, website, and email newsletter to share teasers, behind-the-scenes content, and exclusive updates about the event or book launch.

Utilize Event-specific Hashtags: Create a unique hashtag for your event and encourage attendees to use it when posting on social media. This helps increase online visibility and allows you to track and engage with event-related conversations.

Collaborate with Influencers or Local Partners: Partner with influencers or local businesses that align with your book's genre or target audience. They can help promote the event to their followers or even participate as guest speakers or panelists, adding value and attracting a larger audience.

Offer Exclusive Content or Promotions: Provide attendees with exclusive content, such as sneak peeks of upcoming books, limited edition merchandise, or special discounts. This creates a sense of exclusivity and incentivizes attendance.

Engage with Attendees: Interact with attendees during the event to create a memorable experience. Encourage them to share their thoughts, take photos, and tag your social media accounts. Consider setting up interactive activities or discussion panels related to the themes of your book.

Capture User-Generated Content: Encourage attendees to share their experiences on social media by incorporating designated photo opportunities or selfie stations. Display live social media feeds or curated posts during the event to showcase attendee engagement and generate online buzz.

Live Stream the Event: Consider live streaming parts of your event or book launch for those who couldn't attend in person. Platforms like Facebook Live, Instagram Live, or YouTube Live allow you to reach a wider audience and engage with virtual attendees through real-time comments and interactions.

Offer Signed Copies and Personalized Messages: Make your book launch or event special by offering signed copies of your book. Personalize the signing experience by writing personalized messages or dedications to readers, creating a lasting memory for them.

Follow Up and Maintain Engagement: After the event or book launch, stay engaged with attendees and maintain the momentum. Send follow-up emails thanking attendees for their support and providing links to purchase your book or access exclusive content. Encourage them to share their reviews and experiences on social media.

Leverage Event Highlights for Ongoing Promotion: Use the content and highlights from the event or book launch to continue promoting your book online. Share photos, videos, or testimonials from attendees on social media platforms, website blogs, or email newsletters to keep the buzz alive.

Remember to track the success of your event or book launch through metrics such as attendance, social media engagement, book sales, and audience feedback. This data will help you evaluate the effectiveness of your strategies and guide future event planning and promotional efforts.

Building A Holistic Book Marketing Strategy

Building a holistic book marketing strategy involves incorporating various elements and channels to maximize your book's visibility and reach your target audience. Here are key components to consider when developing a holistic book marketing strategy:

Define Your Target Audience: Identify the specific demographic, interests, and preferences of your ideal readers. This understanding will help you tailor your marketing efforts to reach and engage with them effectively.

Develop a Strong Author Brand: Establish a cohesive author brand that aligns with your book's genre, themes, and target audience. Consistently communicate your brand's voice, values, and personality across all marketing channels.

Online Presence: Create a robust online presence by developing an author website, author blog, and active social media profiles. Regularly update your platforms with engaging content, share insights, and interact with your audience.

Content Marketing: Provide valuable content related to your book's themes or genre through blog posts, articles, videos, or podcasts. This positions you as an expert in your field and attracts readers who are interested in your book's subject matter.

Engage with Readers: Actively engage with your readers through social media, email newsletters, and blog comments. Respond to their questions, thank them for their support, and encourage discussions around your book or related topics.

Book Reviews and Testimonials: Encourage readers to leave reviews and testimonials for your book on platforms like Goodreads, Amazon, or your website. Positive reviews can influence potential readers' purchasing decisions.

Influencer Collaborations: Collaborate with influencers or book bloggers in your genre to promote your book. They can provide reviews, host giveaways, or feature you as a guest on their platforms, reaching their established audience.

Book Launch and Events: Organize book launch events, author signings, or speaking engagements to create buzz around your book. Utilize both online and offline promotion to generate excitement and attract attendees.

Media Outreach: Pitch your book to local media outlets, podcasts, blogs, or book reviewers. Seek opportunities for interviews, guest posts, or feature stories to gain broader exposure for your book.

Email Marketing: Build an email list of interested readers and nurture relationships by sending regular newsletters with updates, exclusive content, and promotions. Use email marketing to stay connected and encourage repeat purchases or engagement.

Cross-Promotion: Collaborate with other authors in your genre to cross-promote each other's books. This can include joint giveaways, guest blogging, or featuring each other in newsletters or social media posts.

Advertising and Promotions: Consider targeted online advertising, such as social media ads or pay-per-click campaigns, to reach a wider audience. Use promotional strategies like limited-time discounts, free chapters, or exclusive bonuses to incentivize readers to purchase your book.

Book Awards and Contests: Submit your book for relevant awards and contests within your genre. Recognition or winning awards can boost credibility and attract the attention of readers, media, and industry professionals.

Continuous Learning and Adaptation: Stay updated on industry trends, marketing techniques, and reader preferences. Continually evaluate the performance of your marketing strategies and make adjustments based on insights and data.

Remember, building a holistic book marketing strategy requires a mix of online and offline efforts, a strong author brand, consistent engagement with your audience, and ongoing adaptation based on feedback and results. Tailor your marketing approach to align with your book's unique characteristics and your target readers' preferences for the best chance of success.

EPILOGUE

As we come to the end of exploring strategies for social media success, it is essential to reflect on the lessons learned and the path ahead. The digital world continues to evolve, presenting authors with new challenges and opportunities.

In this epilogue, we take a moment to celebrate your progress and accomplishments. You have embraced the power of social media, honed your online presence, and established meaningful connections with readers. Your journey has been marked by growth, resilience, and a commitment to embracing the ever-changing world of digital marketing.

Remember that social media success is not an endpoint but an ongoing process. As you continue your author journey, adaptability and continuous learning will be your greatest allies. Stay informed about emerging trends, experiment with new strategies, and remain open to innovative approaches that can further enhance your online presence.

Moreover, never lose sight of the importance of authenticity and genuine connection. Your readers are your most valuable asset, and cultivating meaningful relationships with them will always be at the core of your success. Take the time to engage with your audience, listen to their feedback, and show appreciation for their support. Remember that social media is not solely about self-promotion but about building a community centered around your shared passion for literature.

I want to congratulate you on your dedication and determination throughout this journey. By implementing the strategies outlined in this book, you have positioned yourself for continued growth and success in the digital world. Your commitment to excellence and your willingness to adapt to the ever-changing social media world will serve you well in the years to come.

As you close this book and embark on the next chapter of your author journey, always remember that social media is just one tool in your arsenal. Your talent, creativity, and dedication to your craft are the true foundations of your success. Leverage the power of social media to amplify your voice, expand your reach, and connect with readers in ways that were once unimaginable.

Thank you for joining me on this transformative journey through "Strategies for Social Media Success: Maximizing Your Online Presence." I wish you continued growth, fulfillment, and endless possibilities as you understand the dynamic world of social media and make your mark as an influential author.

Dean Garman

AFTERWORD

As we conclude our exploration of social media strategies for authors, I want to express my gratitude for taking this journey with me. Throughout this book, we have uncovered the immense potential of social media in elevating your online presence and expanding your reach as an author.

Social media is a dynamic and ever-evolving world, and it is essential to approach it with an open mind and a willingness to adapt. As you implement the strategies and techniques discussed in this book, remember that success may not come overnight. Building a strong presence and engaging with your audience takes time and dedication.

In the afterword, I want to leave you with a few final thoughts and reminders as you continue your author journey:

Stay true to yourself: Authenticity is key in the world of social media. Your unique voice and perspective are what will attract readers and keep them engaged. Don't be afraid to showcase your personality and share your passions.

Embrace the power of storytelling: Social media provides an incredible platform to tell your story beyond the pages of your books. Share glimpses into your writing process, behind-the-scenes moments, and personal anecdotes that resonate with your audience.

Build a community: Social media is not just a promotional tool; it is an opportunity to connect with fellow authors and engage with readers who share your love for literature. Foster a sense of community by participating in conversations, supporting other writers, and celebrating literary achievements.

Continuously learn and adapt: Social media platforms are constantly evolving, introducing new features and algorithms. Stay informed about the latest trends and best practices, and be willing to adjust your strategies accordingly to maximize your impact.

Balance promotion with value: While it is important to promote your books, remember to provide value to your audience beyond self-promotion. Share helpful tips, insights, and resources related to your writing genre or topics of interest to your readers.

I hope that the strategies, tips, and insights shared in this book have empowered you to understand the social media world with confidence and purpose. Remember that your online presence is an extension of your author brand, and with dedication and strategic engagement, you can create meaningful connections with readers and amplify your impact as a writer.

Thank you for joining me on this journey, and I wish you great success in leveraging social media to maximize your online presence. May your words reach far and wide, touching the hearts and minds of readers around the world.

Best wishes,

Dean Garman

ACKNOWLEDGEMENTS

Writing a book is a collaborative effort, and I am grateful for the support and contributions of many individuals who have helped bring this project to fruition. I would like to express my heartfelt gratitude to the following people:

First and foremost, I want to thank my family for their unwavering support and encouragement throughout this writing journey. Your love and belief in me have been a constant source of inspiration.

I extend my deepest appreciation to my editor, whose keen insights and constructive feedback have shaped this book into its best possible form. Your expertise and dedication to refining the content have been invaluable.

I would also like to thank my beta readers and critique partners, who provided valuable feedback during the early stages of this book. Your thoughtful input and honest opinions have helped me strengthen the ideas presented within these pages.

To my friends and fellow authors, thank you for your camaraderie and for being a source of motivation and inspiration. Your support and shared experiences have enriched my understanding of the challenges and triumphs in the world of social media for authors.

I am grateful to the publishing team at ANish Publications for their belief in this project and for their meticulous attention to detail in bringing this book to life. Your professionalism and expertise have been instrumental in making this book a reality.

A special thank you goes to the readers who have embraced my previous works and have expressed their support and encouragement. Your enthusiasm fuels my passion for writing and sharing knowledge with fellow authors.

Lastly, I want to express my appreciation to all the authors who have paved the way in the world of social media success. Your insights and experiences have served as a guiding light, and I am grateful for the collective wisdom you have shared.

To all those who have played a role in this book's journey, whether big or small, thank you for your contributions. It is because of your support that this book has come to fruition.

Sincerely,

Dean Garman

ABOUT THE AUTHOR

Dean Garman

 Dean Garman is an accomplished author, marketing strategist, and digital media expert. With a passion for empowering authors, Dean has dedicated his career to helping writers understand the ever-changing world of the publishing industry and maximize their online presence.

With a background in marketing and a deep understanding of the power of social media, Dean has successfully guided numerous authors in building their author brands, connecting with readers, and amplifying their book reach. He brings a unique blend of creativity, strategic thinking, and practical knowledge to his work, enabling authors to understand the digital world with confidence and purpose.

Dean's own journey as an author has provided him with firsthand experience in the challenges and opportunities that arise in the publishing world. His books have resonated with readers around the globe, and his insights have been sought after by both aspiring and established authors alike.

As a sought-after speaker and workshop facilitator, Dean has shared his expertise at conferences, writing events, and online platforms. His dynamic and engaging approach to teaching has inspired countless authors to embrace the potential of social media and leverage it to achieve their writing goals.

When he's not writing or helping authors succeed, Dean enjoys exploring new bookstores, immersing himself in a wide range of literary genres, and spending time in nature for inspiration. He believes in the power of storytelling and the ability of books to create connections and ignite imagination.

With "Strategies for Social Media Success: Maximizing Your Online Presence," Dean Garman continues his mission to empower authors in exploring the digital world. His passion for supporting authors shines through his work, and his commitment to excellence is evident in every page of his books.

Connect with Dean on social media and join the vibrant community of authors who are discovering the transformative power of social media under his guidance. Together, let us unlock the potential of the digital world and elevate your writing career to new heights.

To learn more about Dean Garman and his work, visit his website at www.deangarman.com.

THE AUTHOR'S MARKETING MASTERY SERIES

Welcome to "The Author's Marketing Mastery Series: Empowering Your Book's Success," a comprehensive collection of ten books designed to equip authors with the knowledge, strategies, and tools they need to take control of their book marketing journey.

•From keywords and social media success to creating an engaging online hub with a captivating author website, this series covers every aspect of modern book marketing.
•Look deep into advanced keyword research techniques and discover how to crack the code for optimal visibility.
•Learn the art of adapting your book for the screen and explore the power of reviews in building buzz and credibility.
•Expand your reach beyond borders with international marketing and translation strategies, and harness the potential of paid advertising to boost your book sales.
•Unlock the world of collaborative marketing by partnering with influencers and authors in your genre.
•Finally, master the algorithms of the largest online bookstore, Amazon, to maximize your book's visibility and potential.

With expert guidance, practical tips, and proven strategies, "The Author's Marketing Mastery Series" is your essential companion on the path to success as an author in the competitive publishing industry. Embrace the power of discoverability, engage with readers online, and build a strong brand that captivates audiences worldwide. Empower your book's success and take your author career to new heights with this transformative series.

Discoverability Unleashed: Harnessing Keywords For Effective Book Marketing

Discoverability Unleashed: Harnessing Keywords for Effective Book Marketing" is a game-changing resource for authors looking to enhance their book's discoverability in search results. In this comprehensive guide, you will learn how to leverage relevant keywords to optimize your book's visibility and connect with your target audience.

Strategies For Social Media Success: Maximizing Your Online Presence

Building upon the foundation of book marketing, this book looks into the world of social media. It provides authors with practical tips and proven strategies to leverage various social media platforms effectively. With expert guidance, authors will learn how to engage with readers, cultivate an online following, and ultimately amplify their book's reach in the digital world.

Optimizing Your Author Website: Creating An Engaging Online Hub

A well-designed and engaging author website is crucial for establishing an online presence. In this book, authors will discover the key elements required to create a captivating website that serves as a hub for their literary work. From optimizing user experience to crafting compelling content, this guide equips authors with the tools to create an attractive online destination for readers and potential fans.

Cracking The Code: Advanced Techniques For Keyword Research

This advanced guide takes authors deeper into the world of keyword research, offering them sophisticated techniques to uncover hidden opportunities. By exploring the nuances of keyword analysis, authors will gain a competitive edge in optimizing their book's visibility and discoverability across various online platforms.

From Page To Screen: Adapting Your Book For Film And Television

For authors with ambitions beyond the written word, this book provides a comprehensive roadmap for adapting their books into captivating film or television productions. From understanding the adaptation process to collaborating with industry professionals, this guide unlocks the secrets to successfully bringing stories from the page to the screen.

The Power Of Reviews: Building Buzz And Credibility For Your Book

In this book, authors will explore the influential role that reviews play in generating buzz and establishing credibility for their books. Authors will learn how to strategically obtain and leverage reviews, navigate review platforms, and build a positive reputation that attracts new readers and boosts sales.

Expanding Your Reach: International Marketing And Translation Strategies

To thrive in a global market, authors must understand the

intricacies of international marketing and translation. This book equips authors with the knowledge and tools to effectively promote their books in different languages and cultures, enabling them to expand their reach and connect with readers around the world.

Paid Advertising Demystified: Boosting Book Sales With Strategic Ads

Paid advertising can be a powerful tool for authors looking to enhance their book sales. In this guide, authors will learn the ins and outs of strategic advertising campaigns, including selecting the right platforms, crafting compelling ad copy, and optimizing campaigns for maximum impact. Uncover the secrets to leveraging paid advertising effectively and achieving significant results.

Collaborative Marketing: Working With Influencers And Authors In Your Genre

Collaboration is a valuable strategy for authors seeking to expand their reach and tap into new audiences. This book explores the world of collaborative marketing, guiding authors on how to identify and partner with influencers and fellow authors in their genre. Discover the benefits of collaborative efforts and harness the power of collective promotion.

Mastering Amazon Algorithms: Maximizing Your Book's Visibility

Amazon's algorithms can significantly impact an author's success in the online marketplace. In this final installment of the series, authors will delve into the intricacies of Amazon's algorithms and learn effective strategies to optimize their book's visibility on the platform. Unlock the secrets to maximizing discoverability and boosting sales on the world's largest online bookstore.

www.ingramcontent.com/pod-product-compliance
Lightning Source LLC
LaVergne TN
LVHW051240050326
832903LV00028B/2489